W9-CJG-450

conditions
of love

the philosophy of intimacy

conditions
of love

JOHN ARMSTRONG

W. W. NORTON & COMPANY · *New York* · *London*

First published in Great Britain 2002 by Allen Lane, The Penguin Press,
a publishing division of Penguin Books Ltd
Copyright © 2002 by John Armstrong
First American edition 2003

For information about permission to reproduce selections from this
book, write to Permissions, W. W. Norton & Company, Inc., 500 Fifth
Avenue, New York, NY 10110

Manufacturing by Quebecor Fairfield
Production manager: Julia Druskin

W. W. Norton & Company, Inc.
500 Fifth Avenue, New York, N.Y. 10110
www.wwnorton.com

W. W. Norton & Company Ltd.
Castle House, 75/76 Wells Street, London W1T 3QT

1 2 3 4 5 6 7 8 9 0

contents

the romantic vision

'What is it to love another person?' This is to raise one of the deepest, and most puzzling, questions we can put to ourselves. Love is a central theme in the autobiography we each write as we try to understand our lives; but we may feel that we become only more confused the more we reflect upon it. Love is closely connected with our vision of happiness; yet there is no one we are more likely to hurt, or be hurt by, than the person we love. If love is something we all want, why is it so hard to find and harder to keep? Love is one of humanity's most persistent and most esteemed ideals, but it is hard to say exactly what this ideal is and how – if at all – it relates to real life.

A decisive moment in the history of thinking about love occurred in 1774. This was the year in which Goethe's first novel, *The Sorrows of the Young Werther*, appeared and quickly achieved an overwhelming success throughout Europe. This short book presented a simple, and seductive, vision of the nature of love: love is a feeling. It is still, in its basic elements, the dominant vision of love today. The novel tells the story of Werther's unhappy love for Charlotte; but it was not the plot so much as the intimate description of the development of Werther's passion which excited readers. The experience of love has, of course, always been a literary theme. But this was the first work to take the detailed, systematic account of what it feels like to be in love as its sole theme. Its description of being in love is still immediately recognizable. Love, according to this view, is a sequence of special and intense emotions.

Werther is engulfed by a *longing* to be continually with Charlotte:

'I shall see her today,' I exclaim with delight when I rise in the morning, and look out with gladness of heart at the bright, beautiful sun. 'I shall see her today' and then I have no further wish to form; all – all is included in that one thought.

He is *enraptured* by contact with her:

How my heart beats when by accident I touch her finger, or my feet meet hers under the table! I draw back as from a furnace, but a secret force impels me forward again. Sometimes when we are talking she lays her hand upon mine and in the eagerness of conversation comes closer to me and her balmy breath reaches my lips, – when I feel as if lightning had struck me and that I could sink into the earth.

He is *tormented* by doubt: Does she love me? Is my love returned? Werther describes a moment of extreme anxiety when Charlotte takes leave of him and various others after a party:

I watched Charlotte's eyes, they wandered from one to another but they did not light on me – on me who stood there motionless, and who saw nothing but her. Her carriage drove off and my eyes filled with tears. I looked after her; suddenly I saw Charlotte's bonnet leaning out of the window and she turned to look – was it at me? Perhaps she turned to look at me. Perhaps.

Charlotte is always on his mind; everything else seems trivial. His beloved *is the only important thing in his life* – love is the origin of all value and beauty, without it his world is barren:

What is the world to our hearts without love? What is a magic lantern without light?

These four kinds of intense experience: longing, rapture, doubt and the sense that one is in touch with the source of all value, define the romantic vision of love. I don't mean to suggest that before 1774 people hadn't had such passions – obviously the success of the book depended upon the fact that many people could identify with its hero. The point is just that, at that date, Goethe's novel brought romantic passion into focus as a highly distinctive and important kind of experience. Goethe didn't invent romantic love, he merely provided an unforgettable, exact rendition of the motions of the heart which constitute such love.

It is surely no accident that Werther's love is not returned. When he meets Charlotte she is already engaged, and emotionally attached, to an admirable and attractive man. This obstacle to the progress of love is central to the story. Werther eventually shoots himself: he is unable to live without Charlotte and she is unavailable. But her unavailability plays a more subtle role as well. Werther has no possibility of bringing his love to fruition. He cannot marry Charlotte, or live with her. He cannot even express his love without upsetting and compromising her. So his passion remains in a pristine state. His longings are never converted into satiety. He is desperate to see her – but never finds out what it would be like to have to see her every day. He is excited when their feet touch accidentally; but the excitement depends partly upon the fact that their feet are not supposed to meet under the table. Would the intensity remain if he could touch her whenever he liked?

Unreciprocated and thwarted love play an important part in the romantic vision just because they prevent passion being fulfilled; they maintain it at its highest pitch. They are seen not as failures of love but as the most perfect instances of love. The story of Romeo and Juliet is a key instance of romantic love for the same reason. Death, after a single night together, prevents the couple from having to sustain their mutual passion. They cannot become bored or stale; they cannot discover irritating habits or annoying characteristics in each other; they do not have to confront any differences of opinion or taste.

The romantic conception of love focuses our attention on the opening moments of a relationship. It regards falling in love as the essence of love. In this sense love involves an excited preoccupation with the loved one and delight in their presence. It is marked by a vivid conviction that the other is the key to one's happiness. When two people fall in love, they move very rapidly to a feeling of intimacy; the ordinary barriers of reserve suddenly come down. Isolation is overcome and there is a blissful closeness. This love, of course, tends to be relatively short-lived. It may last, in its full brightness, for a few days, weeks or months. It is only prolonged beyond this when the beloved is absent or inaccessible. While it lasts we are 'in love' – we are overcome by our passion. Because this is such a dazzling experience and because it is concerned with such extremes of delight and despair, it is hardly surprising that it should be the first thing which comes to mind when we think of love.

To an eighteenth-century reader Werther was an unusual and exciting figure because of the intensity of his feelings. He belonged to an 'aristocracy of sentiment' – separated from the mass of humanity by the depth and self-consciousness of his passions. He stood out in contrast to the courtly culture of artifice and calculation, as well as to the common sense and restraint of the middle class. It is a mark of the success of Romanticism that such feelings – once imagined to be the province only of a spiritual élite – are widespread today. The capacity for romantic passion appears now to be a common denominator of modern human nature. It is just this universality which reveals a special feature of the romantic view of love. Nothing is required for love except a willing heart – an openness to feeling. And there is nothing we are more willing to recognize in ourselves than our own tenderness. In so far as we regard ourselves as capable of feeling we regard ourselves as capable of love. Love, in other words, has only one condition: passion. And everyone can satisfy this condition. The romantic view sponsors a completely democratic conception of love.

We want love to last. But the romantic vision concentrates only on the opening stages of an encounter with another person. It focuses our attention on how relationships start but doesn't tell us how they continue once the initial bloom has passed. In fact the romantic emphasis on passion distorts one's view of the long term. When passion diminishes it looks, on this view, as if love is declining. The later part of the relationship is just the after-glow of the genuine period of love. Or, if there are difficulties later on, the assumption is that to revive love we have to try to return to the glory of the early days. However sweet this is as an idea, it may well distract our attention from a more important point. Perhaps long-term love doesn't really resemble romantic love very much. Falling in love is, obviously, an important aspect of love. But to elevate the beginning of a relationship is to do an injustice to its future – it provides a misleading model for thinking about love. Love is a process which develops and changes over time. So a description of what is going on at a later stage may look very different from an account of the start. To judge the whole of a process by the experience of the beginning is the mark of immaturity.

Our collective understanding of love is beguiled by love's first moments; and yet it is continuing, long-term love that we all want. Real love is love that lasts and withstands the difficulties which a prolonged relationship inevitably brings. The problems of love occur not when passion is rejected or when fate intervenes to cut off a relationship at the earliest stage. It is, ironically, when we are loved back, when a relationship develops, that love is put to the test. It is the long term that we want to understand; we are in search of a mature conception of love.

'love is really *x*'

We might suppose that if we are to understand love, if we are to come to a mature perspective upon it, we should start by trying to define the central term. That is, we should start by trying to sum up in a single, precise sentence what love is. Just as, if we were hoping to understand the role of art in life, we might start by trying to define art. And, indeed, there have been many attempts to say what love is. These range from the wildly poetic: 'love is the growth of the wings of the soul', to the cynical: 'love is an illusion'; from the optimistic: 'love is the solution to the deepest problems of existence', to the deflationary: 'love is friendship plus sex'.

However intriguing or suggestive these statements may be, none is very impressive as a definition. A good definition tells us exactly what the thing in question is. For example, the scientific definition of gold – expressed in terms of atomic structure – lays bare the essence of gold. It tells us precisely what makes gold different from other metals and explains why gold has the observable properties it does. Gold is malleable, heavy and yellow because of its atomic structure. This is the hidden common factor, the *x*, which all gold things have in common. A definition which captures this underlying factor has great explanatory power.

The various definitions of love, however, are not nearly so successful when judged by this standard. And we might wonder why we haven't been able to come up with a good definition of love. Is it because love, like God, is too mysterious, too subtle or too ineffable to be comprehended in words? Are we too stupid to grasp the real, essential nature of love? Unfortunately, for those attracted to mysteries, there is a simpler explanation to hand: an explanation, that is, of why we have been unable to define love. The explanation was suggested by Wittgenstein in the *Philosophical Investigations*. There, Wittgenstein directs our attention to the way we use a whole range of ordinary words, taking the word 'game' as his prime example. His point is that we can't actually give a satisfactory definition of even this simple word. If, for instance, we suggest that games always have a competitive character, as chess and football do, someone will point out that sex games and solo card games don't have winners or losers. If we try again and suggest that games always involve rules, it will be replied that children's games of make-believe do not follow rules. The word 'game' can't be adequately defined; yet this is not because there is something mystical or spiritual about games. It is not that games really do have an essential nature which we are somehow unable to grasp. Instead, the explanation goes as follows. We are tempted to assume that there is a common factor which links all things called by a single term. The aim of definition would then be to reveal this common factor. When we fail to come up with a definition we are led to suppose that this is because the common factor eludes us: it exists, only we can't pin it down.

What Wittgenstein does is put into question the under-lying assumption. Perhaps there isn't always a common factor x which unites all the things we call by the same name. Perhaps the variety of relationships and attachments we dignify with the term 'love' don't share a single, common nature. Perhaps the goal of trying to define this common nature is fundamentally misconceived.

The fact that we can't define a word does not mean that its use is random or chaotic. Think a little more about the way we use the word 'game'. We don't call things games because they participate in a subtle essence of 'gamehood'. However, games do exhibit various kinds of 'family resemblance', as Wittgenstein put it. For example, children play make-believe games for fun. That they are played for fun is something they have in common with activities such as chess and football. Part of the point of calling these activities games is to stress this aspect of enjoyment. However, if an army classifies its practice manoeuvres as a game, this is not because they are having fun but because they are conducting a make-believe battle, rather than a real one. There is a resemblance, here, with respect to the 'not for real' aspect.

Although we can trace various patterns of resemblance which hold between the things we call games, there isn't a single way in which they all resemble each other. This is exactly the way physical characteristics occur in families. Two children may both resemble their mother and yet not resemble each other because they have inherited different features of her appearance. If the word 'love' functions in parallel to the word 'game', this would explain why we can't define love – why it doesn't have an essence. The explanation, however, would focus on how language works rather than on the supposed super-subtle and ineffable qualities of love.

Certainly, when we consider the love of chocolate, of freedom, God's love for the world, romantic passion and maternal care, it seems plausible to suppose that the word 'love' has a different import when it is used to refer to these different things. The love of chocolate does not seem to share a subtle essence with maternal love and neither of these seems to be the same as romantic love. When it comes to chocolate, 'love' functions as an extreme version of 'like'. And this isn't strange because often we do like the people we love. Nevertheless, there are important cases in which 'love' doesn't stress liking but something else – for example, loyalty. And it would be a mistake to insist that there just has to be some hidden common factor which always unites liking and loyalty. The fact is that we can use a single word, 'love', now for one, then later for another, aspect of attachment.

This account of how the word 'love' functions coheres with an understanding of its history or, more accurately, of the group of words the varied meanings of which have contributed to the use of our present term. For example, the modern English word 'love' has inherited the significations of the words it has been used to translate. When Ovid and Horace write of *amor* what they have in mind is a highly sexualized attachment; not just lust but a kind of romantic lust. When the Vulgate Bible speaks of *caritas* it indicates unselfish goodwill towards another person. Yet both of these terms are translated by 'love'. This is not because we have discovered some unexpected factor which is common to *amor* and *caritas*. It is just that we can use a single term to designate more than one kind of experience or attitude.

The discussion of language has implications for an investigation of love. When we considered games we saw that there were various themes, such as enjoyment or make-believe, which are at work in different uses of the term 'game'. So, too, with love. Love doesn't have an essence that we can uncover; it has, rather, a set of themes that interact differently in different instances of love. This book is built round the idea that love is thematic, in two ways. Firstly, the task of thinking about love is understood as the task of separating the many themes, the many strands of thought, that are entangled around our word 'love'. Secondly, the idea that love isn't a single thing but a complex of different concerns gives rise to a vision of some of the problems of love. When we try to love we are not actually trying to undertake a single endeavour; rather, we are trying to do a whole range of different, and sometimes not very compatible, things simultaneously. This helps, for example, to focus our view of the limitations of Werther's experience of love. It is not that the romantic conception of love as a sequence of intense emotions is straightforwardly false. The problem is, rather, that it concentrates on only one theme of love: the theme of feeling. Hence it ignores the other strands of experience that are relevant to an adequate conception of love. And it is these other strands that we have to pay attention to if we are to come to a mature vision of love.

3

love's evolution

One of the most basic questions we can ask about any kind of human activity or experience, including love, concerns purpose: what is it for? Currently the most powerful way of formulating such a question does not focus on the present. It does not ask: what is love for today? Rather it makes inquiry into the distant past of humanity and asks: what role, if any, did love play in the lives of our prehistorical ancestors? Evolutionary psychology proposes that the basic structures and propensities of the human mind as they are exhibited in the modern world were laid down in the millennia between the emergence of the human species and the waning of the last ice age. The subsequent period, a hundred or so generations, is too short to have much evolutionary significance.

Evolution is the record of reproductive success. We have inherited the genetic material of those individuals who managed to reproduce in the face of competition from other humans and against the hostile forces of the environment they inhabited. Evolution is also the story of unintended success. Human beings, it is true, have survived partly because of such things as their ability to make fires and fashion tools. But knowing how to make bonfires or bows and arrows is not a genetic endowment. We are not born with an understanding of these things; we are born only with the kinds of minds and bodies which are, in principle, able to cope with such undertakings. Human beings obviously had this potential long before they deliberately mastered the arts of survival. The potential itself must have emerged, as all genetic development does, in a complex sequence of accidents. Genes, obviously, do not observe the world and assess what kind of mutation or development would further their reproductive aims. Genetic material simply is prone to mutation and no one has had any conscious control over the direction of mutation until the last years of the last century. Almost always the mutation of genetic material makes no difference to the resulting organism or leads to some defect or infirmity. However, very occasionally mutation causes the organism to behave in a way that, fortuitously, enhances its chances of successful reproduction. If the offspring inherit this genetic reproduction, which increases their chances of successful reproduction, they will in turn pass on the same material to their descendants. Since these individuals are marginally more successful in reproducing than those around them, this genetic material and the kind of behaviour which it promotes will come to be characteristic of the species. Although, of course, this will take an extremely long time to happen.

One of the most extraordinary claims of evolutionary psychology has been that the capacity and tendency to experience love is part of our genetic endowment. The structure of our minds is set for love. Such a claim, if it is to have credibility, has to be able to meet two challenges.

Firstly, it must be able to explain how a disposition to such a complex set of intentions and reactions could be built into the mind. The claim that it is has benefited greatly from the rise of cognitive science, which undertakes to show how extremely complex emotions and thoughts are enacted in material processes. It makes it plausible to think that the detailed architecture of the brain governs the way a human being feels and thinks. In so far as genetic material determines the brain's architecture, it can thereby determine the kinds of thoughts and feelings to which we are prone. It therefore makes sense to claim that the capacity to love and the tendency to experience love could be genetically inherited. The first challenge to the evolutionary thesis can be adequately met.

This, however, does nothing to show that such a disposition is part of the standard genetic inheritance of a modern human being. So, a second challenge to the genetic thesis arrives: how could a tendency to experience love have conferred a reproductive benefit on our remote ancestors, a benefit sufficient to ensure that this endowment would eventually come to predominate in the species?

The response to this challenge is necessarily speculative. We do not actually know very much about the emotional or social lives of our remote ancestors. What we can do, however, is attempt to reconstruct the reproductive difficulties they were under and to show the benefits which would have followed from the unintentional evolution of certain capacities and tendencies – those which we think of as related to love. The reproductive condition of early humanity, prior to the emergence of love, might be described in the following terms. Males seek to mate with as many females as possible, but they are especially drawn to those females who have the secondary characteristics of fertility and health: clear skin, long hair, well-formed breasts and hips. Such attraction is involuntary. The males who didn't have such a focus for their desires mated with unhealthy and infertile women and left fewer descendants who, inheriting this lack of discrimination, in turn left even fewer. Of course, access to such prime women would be the preserve of the most powerful males. Females, by contrast, would instinctively try to reserve their reproductive efforts for the most powerful males. Again, this is imagined as an involuntary reaction, not as a calculation. Females who didn't have this instinct would have weaker offspring less able, in their turn, to reproduce successfully. Grim though it appears, this ruthless arrangement nevertheless provides an opening for love.

Successful reproduction, obviously, does not just depend upon the art of procreation. For an individual's genetic inheritance to be passed on, their children must not only be born but must develop in such a way that they, in turn, are well placed to reproduce. The male offspring need to be powerful and the females need to be healthy and fertile. Any mode of parental behaviour that increases the probability of such an outcome therefore enhances the probability of the parents' genetic material being passed to subsequent generations. Any mutation of genetic endowment which led an individual to behave in ways that encouraged the production of successful children would, gradually, become a general characteristic of the species. The central contention here is that loyalty to, and care for, a mate in the period following conception helps to ensure the well-being of the offspring. The male needs to ensure that the mother of his child will be loyal to him and to his child; that she won't mate with another male and devote her attention and nourishment to another man's child. The female needs to be sure that her mate won't abandon her and the child, won't go off and give his protection and support to another partner. The chances of successful reproduction, therefore, are enhanced by character traits in both parents which tend towards enduring loyalty and care; enduring, that is, at least for the period in which a child is most vulnerable and has most to gain from parental support. The thesis proposes that such a characteristic will be structured like lust. That is, it will function as an emotion. This is because emotions guide complex action and are involuntary. The involuntary aspect means that, once it is up and running, the individual is likely to persist in the course of action to which the emotion tends. We are, therefore, looking at the evolution of an emotion which guides one individual to be loyal and caring towards another; this is very close to love. The evolutionary thesis, therefore, claims that we can understand how love could develop as a human characteristic because it has a plausible story about how such an emotion would confer a reproductive benefit on those who experienced it. And, in conjunction with cognitive science, it can plausibly claim that the capacity to feel such an emotion could result from genetic mutation (over a suitably long time) and hence could be an inheritable quality: a feature of the human genetic character.

If we find this account convincing, or even just credible,

we might wonder what light, if any, it sheds upon our understanding of love today. One crucial implication is this: we should expect the alignment of love and lust to differ between the sexes. According to this thesis, a male cannot lose by promiscuity. Even a male who is loyal and devoted to a particular mate may still succeed in leaving more descendants if he also tries to mate with other females. Any children resulting from such encounters will have a lesser chance of survival than the offspring of the female to whom he is devoted. Nevertheless, if any of them do survive that male's genetic material is spread more widely. This point is not meant to suggest a subtle calculation on the part of prehistoric males. All it suggests is that an inheritable tendency to non-promiscuous behaviour would not become dominant in the male sex. Thus, in general, we should expect lust and love to be separable for males. Further, love should, according to the logic of the argument, only occur in the wake of lust. In the prehistorical era a male should only have become attached to a female once he had successfully mated with her.

By contrast, we should expect love and lust to be more closely connected in female experience. Because a female can, in principle, reproduce much less often than a male she should only be attracted to the more powerful males. And her experience of love should, according to the theory, coincide with her experience of lust. That is, we should expect a female to feel lust more or less only for the same partners towards whom she feels love. We should also expect that for females lust will be dependent upon love. For, from an evolutionary point of view, a female will have a better chance of reproducing successfully if she makes herself available only to a mate of whose devotion she is already convinced. Thus, for a female, feeling loved would be a key condition for feeling lust. Again it is important to stress that these statements about what we should expect a woman today to feel are not meant to record deliberate strategies. We are not being asked to imagine prehistoric or modern females working out rationally what will best serve their reproductive aims and then acting accordingly. We are, instead, being asked to imagine a series of involuntary genetic mutations which influence the structure of the brain and which lead to patterns of feeling and conduct over which the individual has no direct control.

A second major implication of the genetic thesis derives from just this involuntary aspect. The thesis suggests that we should regard elements of modern behaviour as deriving not from the conscious personality of the individual but as laid down by genetic inheritance. We should not, therefore, blame men and women, as individuals, for their patterns of conduct, in so far as these are determined genetically. We have, the thesis tells us, less control over how we feel and act than we might like to believe. The basic features of two very different emotional genders were established prior to the emergence of civilization. A fundamental conflict of modern romance, the fact that men more easily separate love and sex than do women, is seen as being a dictate of nature. We need love, we have an inbuilt need to love and be loved, yet the two sexes have divergent notions of how love works. The unhappiness of love is the fault of the evolution of the species. How far should we trust this view of love? That is the question to which we now turn.

why love has a history

The genetic account of love is radically ahistorical. That is, it proposes a universal and constant human nature – of the mind as well as of the body. The broad outline of the genetic inheritance of all people is the same. This makes it look as if love ought to be always and everywhere the same. Such an account may also be thought to support the pessimistic conclusion that there is nothing we can do to ameliorate the problems of love. The two sexes just do have different dispositions and nothing we can do can change that. These conclusions seem enticing to anyone who wants to attack certain liberal assumptions of the late twentieth century. The liberal view puts the blame for the unhappiness of love upon social conditions: the conventions we have adopted, or which have been imposed upon us, lead to misery. These conventions can and should be challenged and changed. The genetic theorist is unimpressed. You can change conventions all you like, but you can't change human nature. But is the position really as simple and depressing as this? If we accept the genetic position, do we have to embrace its universal and pessimistic conclusion?

*

A key question we have to ask concerns the status of what I have been calling inclinations, tendencies and dispositions. The genetic thesis is that dispositions can be inherited. These words mask considerable uncertainty. What is a disposition? It is quite clear that men are not compelled to be promiscuous, nor that women are bound by a law of nature to be highly selective when it comes to finding partners – yet if the genetic thesis is true this must be compatible with a disposition towards promiscuity or selectivity. More blatantly, neither side is even compelled to reproduce – which would, from a logical point of view, have to be a stronger disposition than any that concerned the details of who to reproduce with. So it is clear that if there are such dispositions they must stand in complex relation to other aspects of the mind or personality. And these other aspects of the mind can override or modify dispositions. They can invest dispositions with further significance or meaning – and do so in ways which have no direct bearing upon evolution. For example, lust might be regarded as the prompting of the devil, or as an attack by the body upon the mind; while such ways of thinking do not eradicate a disposition to sexual pleasure they surely have an impact upon behaviour. It may be true that the basic components of the mind have not changed since prehistory; but it is clear that the content of thought has developed dramatically. And the content of thought – how we think about ourselves and our desires – makes a difference to our behaviour.

One area in which there has been exponential development is reflexive thought. It is clear that human beings have increasingly developed special kinds of belief and desire. These are beliefs and desires which focus not upon the world but upon mental items. We have attitudes towards our beliefs and desires. Thus a man may resist an inclination because he thinks it immoral to accord with it; another may endorse and cultivate the same disposition because he thinks it noble. While such reflexive attitudes and 'second-order' beliefs and desires are common to humanity they obviously exhibit two kinds of variation: cultural and individual. Cultures vary in general strategies of rejection and endorsement – a whole society or era might be marked by a desire to control appetite or, perhaps, to achieve consistency amongst beliefs. But individuals will also vary in the strength and character of their reflexive attitudes.

Take just one example. The cult of monasticism in the Middle Ages, which led many of the most able and hence most reproducible males into celibacy and chastity, must have overridden any inherited disposition to reproduction. Further, in this period there wasn't a rejection of love, but on the contrary a massive investment of the notion of love. Only love was directed to God, his laws, his saints – rather than to sexual or romantic concerns. Although this attitude was characteristic of an era and a place it was obviously not possessed in equal measure by all individuals.

This example points to two crucial kinds of transformation which can take place in relation to a disposition. A disposition can be set aside at the level of action, even though it may continue to exert some kind of pull on one's desires. The point is this: desires don't automatically guide action; they only guide action in connection with a surrounding set of beliefs and in concert with – or opposition to – other desires.

A second transformation concerns the way a disposition is interpreted. A distinction between sexual desire and love, to pursue the theme, builds upon many other features of intellectual culture. It derives from a vision of human nature – for example the belief that the soul is not sexual, that the soul is 'in the body, but not of the body'. It may depend upon a vision of the relation between God and the world – or theodicy, as it is called. According to the Christian view, sex played an important part in the fall of man from God's grace; the central act of redemption – the birth and death of Christ – was motivated by love. 'God so loved the world that he sent his only son to be our saviour.' In this climate of belief the significance of love is very highly charged. So, whatever the underlying disposition defined by evolutionary psychology, the experience of the individual is going to be heavily inflected by culture. People won't stop having sexual desires but their experience of what sex is and how it relates to – or stands opposed to – love isn't dependent on their genetic inheritance. Rather it derives from a general, schematic view of just about everything else.

This is why love has a history. The experience of love – what it is like to love and be loved – will depend upon features of the culture and the individual. Therefore despite the common inherited dispositions identified by evolutionary psychology, we have to recognize that the experience of love changes as the surrounding culture of beliefs changes, particularly the beliefs which articulate what we think another person is, what we think is good or right, what we think our duties to ourselves are. Thus, if we believe the evolutionary account we should still recognize the limits of its explanatory power – its power to tell us, today, what love is and what it is for.

Suppose we take an actual historical case of love such as Dante's love for Beatrice – the love which is woven so deeply into *The Divine Comedy* – and ask what that love was. The evolutionary answer that it was a genetically inherited strategy for reproduction isn't going to sound like a plausible answer – even if we accept that Dante would have had such a genetic inheritance. The significance of love was dependent upon all his other beliefs about himself, about God and about the world.

When we consider a case like Dante's we are powerfully reminded of the reasons which have supported a view of love quite contrary to that advocated by evolutionary psychology. Love, it is suggested, is a cultural construct; and the way it is constructed depends upon various features of a given society. For example, in a society such as ours in which adults very often live alone until they fall in love, love is closely connected to overcoming loneliness. But this could hardly be a major feature of the experience of love in a society in which – until marriage – the individual would normally live in the closest proximity to an extended family. Again, in periods when the roles of men and women are closely defined and completely distinct, love – which draws a man and woman together – will be envisaged through these roles. In a time when there is no such clear distinction, or where distinctions are grounds of tension and dispute, the experience of what it is to love will change too. What it is to care for the well-being of another person depends upon what you suppose constitutes the well-being of that person. The evolutionary account stresses the idea that caring for the well-being of another individual (an individual with whom one is sexually active) may be an innate disposition. But depending upon how 'well-being' is understood this may lead to very different patterns of behaviour. In one culture, well-being might be likened to having lots of male children; in another to having a tidy home and meat on the table at five o'clock; in another to cultivating freedom of the spirit. Genetically speaking the same disposition is at work but its impact upon behaviour depends upon the way we think, or what we happen to take for granted, about what is good for ourselves and for other people. And although these beliefs and concerns are framed by our cultural horizons, there is, of course, huge individual variation.

What is the significance of cultural variation with respect to the experience of love? Does it matter, at a personal level, whether one thinks that love is a universal or local phenomenon or some combination of the two – as I have been suggesting? What is the incentive to invest one's belief in either of these positions?

The idea that a kind of feeling is natural and universal can be used to lend dignity to our emotional lives. It is felt that if love is natural it is therefore proper and good, because an equation is made between what is natural and how we should behave. (An equation still manifest in commonplace advice: 'Just be natural.') But this positive evaluation is misleading. The fact that a tendency is universal or natural does not show that we should abide by it. It is almost certainly natural to distrust strangers – and it is quite easy to see how such an attitude could have evolved. It is probably natural to neglect, or even attack, weak infants and direct resources to more healthy children; bitter rivalry amongst siblings seems to be natural. But in none of these cases do we now think that such behaviour is good. We are perfectly able to see that an instinct may no longer serve a good purpose. We are able to evaluate our instincts by reference to their consequences in the world in which we actually live – a world radically different from that in which they were laid down. Therefore to show that love is natural is not in fact to show anything very important. The worth and dignity of love is not ensured because it developed in foraging societies.

What then of enthusiasm for the view that love is not natural? The relativist, liberal claim is sometimes formulated quite aggressively. Love is 'merely' a social construct; it is 'simply' the product of economic and ideological factors. This imports an evaluation: constructs are flimsy, products are tainted. If we put our faith in them we are compromising ourselves. But this negative evaluation is open to question. After all, there is a very different interpretation which could be drawn from the same premises. One might say, for example, that the experience of love has changed over time – and therefore concede that love is not an ahistorical constant. But in saying this one is not necessarily suggesting that love is just a 'convention' – just a made-up set of rules which we could easily dispense with. Love may have changed, but in many ways changed for the better; the possibilities of romantic love, or the personalized, communicative love of a parent for a child, are an achievement of civilization. The evaluation, positive or negative, doesn't follow automatically from the assumption that love isn't a universal phenomenon. There might be wonderful things which require special conditions in order to come into being. The sonata, for example, is obviously the product of particular cultural conditions – but that doesn't reduce the value of Beethoven's efforts in this genre. The fact that it requires education and leisure to read the volumes of Proust doesn't lead to the conclusion that there is something wrong with his novel; it reminds us why we value education and leisure. What is given by nature is not necessarily good, what is achieved by artifice is not necessarily worthless.

The attraction of the liberal position has always been its optimism. It allows one to think that patterns of behaviour are not fixed and that change for the better is possible. Since there have been real changes in the way people conduct their emotional lives it looks as if the liberal position must be, at least, partly true. Yet if we are also persuaded by the genetic thesis we are going to have to accept that not all aspects of the psyche are open to conscious modification. In fact, there is much evidence that suggests that emotional life is at once flexible in some respects and inflexible in others. For example, the twentieth century saw dramatic changes in the sexual self-presentation of women. Female sexuality became much more public and the assumption that men have a duty to please women in bed became a commonplace. Nevertheless, certain things didn't change. Male and female patterns of arousal still seem to be different. Male arousal still seems to be more closely connected with visual stimulation and less closely connected with affection than is female arousal. Some aspects of sexual experience have been open to change, others are intransigent.

When it comes to love we see something similar. Recognition of what the needs of another may be is open to change and progress. We really can become more loving by developing a richer sense of what might be important to another person and by cultivating an interest in finding out what those needs are. On the other hand, emotional structures like jealousy and possessiveness don't seem to change much. It was just this complexity in our nature, governed partly by convention and partly by nature, that eluded the sexual reformers of the 1970s. Having realized that it was only a convention that men should cut their hair short or wear ties, they proceeded to the very different conclusion that sexual possessiveness is also merely a convention and therefore something that can be easily discarded. They tried to understand the whole of the human psyche according to a model derived from fashion. Fashions change regularly but always seem natural to those who follow them. The genetic thesis shows up the flaw in this analogy. With fashion, the goal is to align oneself with a group; changes in fashion are insignificant so long as a whole group changes at the same time. So through changes in fashion the important factor, the relation between individual and group, is constant. However, the emotion of jealousy is not concerned with groups. The desire to hold on to what one has, and to resent it being taken by others, is a self-protective instinct. Various aspects of our conduct have different bases in the mind; this helps explain why they are not equally open to change or reformation. A pattern of change applicable to one field of behaviour can be inapplicable to another. We need to work with two ideas simultaneously: the experience of love is open to change, but only in some ways.

If we accept this premise of limitation, we might still want to know to what extent the experience of love is open to change and to understand the mechanisms by which such change can be brought about. In thinking about dispositions we saw that they need to be fleshed out by our view of the world. A disposition to be nice to another person will govern our behaviour in concert with our sense of what niceness consists of. One of the ordinary tragedies of love occurs when one person is well intentioned and well disposed towards another, but has no adequate idea of how to make the other person happy. It is one thing to feel loving towards someone, another to translate this feeling into words and actions which make the other person feel loved. Love needs to be realized, made substantial, in conduct if it is to be communicated. Although this fact gives rise to many of the problems of love it is also an avenue of hope. For the ways we realize our intentions, the ways we turn them into behaviour, are more open to change than the underlying intentions and dispositions themselves.

People can be better or worse at seeing opportunities to make their affection apparent to the one they love. They can be better or worse at seeing what the needs or problems of the other might be; at recognizing the impact of their own behaviour on the other. This has nothing to do with strength of feeling or intensity of longing. Instead it has everything to do with perceptual acuity and imagination. For it is imagination that allows us to think about how the experience of another may differ from our own;

it allows us to wonder what they might need and to wonder how our behaviour strikes them. Imagination opens up the possibility of asking: How might I do things otherwise? The role of imagination is central to love and is the subject of the central portion of this book. But for the present I want to concentrate on a slightly different issue: the value we place upon our actions and those of others.

To elaborate on this point, consider a painting by Chardin – the *Meal for a Convalescent*, painted around 1747 when Chardin was in his late forties; the picture hangs today in the National Gallery of Art, Washington, DC. The picture shows a middle-aged woman carefully peeling an egg. On a small table, draped in a fine linen cloth, stands the rest of the simple meal. What is striking about the picture is the air of thoughtfulness it creates. We do not see the convalescent; but the woman's patient care is made evident. A generous reaction to the picture will see it as a vision of the way in which love is enacted in small things. Anyone who can identify with this woman's care is drawn into a culture that endorses and helps give value to such actions. Culture – in this case Chardin's pictorial art – helps invest a moment with significance and value. For the painting gives this ordinary, uneventful moment special weight – it picks it out as especially worth attending to and reveals its beauty and grace. With the help of the picture we can see how love may be enacted in the shelling of an egg. But it may take an artist of Chardin's stature and power to reveal this to us.

Thus love has two histories. It has a general history that follows the broad changes of the cultural climate. And love also has an individual history, worked out in the life of each person who comes to love another. This is the history of how we, as individuals, turn inherited dispositions into actual bits of behaviour. It is the way we find, or fail to find, openings for our love in words and actions.

When we pay attention to the variation of love according to time and place, we are really studying the way in which the experience of love depends upon the wider beliefs and concerns within which evolutionary dispositions operate. It is this conjunction which creates the experience of love. And this indicates what it is one has to look at in the attempt to understand one's own experience of love. We have to attend to the surrounding culture of ideas and concerns that provides the arena in which we try to love – in which our genetic dispositions get played out, interpreted, resisted and transformed. Long-term love is always going to be difficult – the evolutionary account reveals that. But the difficulties are also the product of how we think; and how we think is something over which we can at least hope to exercise some benevolent control.

the perfect union

In the beginning – according to the most famous myth of the origin of love – each human being was a 'rounded whole' with two faces, two backs, four arms and four legs. These double creatures were of three types depending on the genders of their component halves: male, female and hermaphrodite. 'Their strength and vigour made them very formidable, and their pride was overweening; they attacked the gods.' To weaken them and put an end to their insolence – but not quite destroy them – Zeus cut them in two. 'If this doesn't keep them quiet I'll bisect them again; they can hop on one leg.' Love is the yearning of each part to find its original partner and return to the original, complete state. The perfect lovers are those who were originally joined together. If they find each other they wish never to be separated and try to merge completely, to become once more the single being they originally were.

This myth, put into the mouth of Aristophanes, is recounted in Plato's *Symposium* – perhaps the most successful philosophical drama we have (the competition has not been too intense). The play presents speeches at a drinking party supposedly given by a young poet to celebrate his triumph at the Athenian festival. Although the speeches are almost exclusively concerned with homosexual relationships they have been widely influential in the Western vision of love in general.

One major theme of this myth is that there is a 'right' person for each of us. If we can only find this person our problems will be over. This is to construe the difficulty of love by analogy with a treasure hunt. Correspondingly, what goes wrong in love always derives from attaching ourselves to the wrong person – or the wrong person getting attached to us. Of course, there is much to be said in favour of this view. Many couples have to separate because they do not see eye to eye on practical matters. One wants to live in a large city, the other longs for the countryside; one likes only antique furniture, the other only modern. In reacting to this one might seek out a partner whose tastes and aspirations perfectly coincide with one's own. This approach is sensibly respectful of fragility. It recognizes that goodwill can founder on deep-set incompatibility. According to this view, the blindness of romantic love consists precisely in the assumption that love will triumph over practicality – that the excitement you feel in the presence of this special person will overcome the fact that you want to live in different countries. Or eat in different kinds of restaurant.

In *Husbands and Wives*, Woody Allen sympathetically caricatures the kind of longing which may be traced to this good sense. 'Spencer was searching for a woman interested in golf, inorganic chemistry, outdoor sex and the music of Bach. In short he was looking for himself, only female.' The painful side of the joke is that this attempt to overcome a problem of love leads to an avoidance of love; the other person is no longer someone else.

This shouldn't be seen as a way of trying to legitimize a kind of narcissistic dream of self-love. The point, surely, is that the other person, in this scenario, is one's own creation – a person whose characteristics are governed by one's own demands.

This scheme of calculated love comes up against certain difficulties. Firstly, the demand for compatibility is never satisfied. The list we make always leaves room for new demands – and hence new ways in which people can turn out to be incompatible. They may wish to live in the same country, the same city, the same house, but if they want to paint the sitting-room walls differently then they may be heading for divorce. When people agree about almost everything, the few points of difference can still seem – to them – enormous. The attempt to foreclose this possibility by seeking more and more perfect compati-bility is self-defeating. In other words, the search for perfect compatibility can be a highly respectable way of not loving. The searcher can say: 'I am loving, I am capable of love, only I haven't found the right person yet', but the 'right person' is specified so closely that they never will find such a person; they will always be disappointed because whoever they find will fall short in some way, will fail to meet one of their requirements. But, in their own eyes, this is not a shortcoming of their own; it is simply bad luck. And what gives this strategy its power is the fact that it shelters behind a very sensible observation: incompatibility often destroys relationships – therefore perfect compatibility must be the right basis. This may look like good logic but is actually fallacious. It is like convincing yourself that because overeating is bad for you, the perfect meal would be a gulp of air.

Avoidance, in fact, is a key characteristic of the search for the 'right person'. Attention is diverted away from the seeker. They have no responsibility to be loving; they imagine that when they do find the right person love will be easy, will flower spontaneously and survive of its own accord. The main thrust of this book is in the opposing direction. What I shall argue is that finding a good enough partner is no guarantee at all that love will flourish. We can easily imagine that if Woody Allen's Spencer finds his ideal mate love will still elude him. The problem is not in finding the person but in finding the resources and capacities in oneself to care for another person – to love them. Searching for the right 'object' diverts attention from finding the right attitude.

A second problem with this attempt to find the 'right person' is that it does not pay enough attention to the ways in which priorities change through a relationship. A woman who has – as she thinks – no interest in having children may, from within a loving relationship, come to have a different view. And here, the ground of the change is the relationship itself. She may have learned, with her partner, to recognize capacities and concerns she did not know she had. The calculation – the picturing of the perfect partner – presupposes that we can enter a relationship with a clear-sighted and complete understanding of our needs and capacities. This is to see a relationship as a kind of garment which merely goes on top of, and does not in any way change, the inner person.

Against this we have to set a comment which is occasionally heard from people who have loved in the long term. In some moods they may be tempted to say that they could have loved someone else. It didn't have to be this person. Perhaps what they have in mind is this: the experience of learning to love someone in the long term involves various adaptations of oneself to the other; it involves dropping certain demands, learning others, changing priorities. But if you are able to do this with one person you would probably have been able to do it with another – at least with some others. Compatibility, on this view, is an achievement of love, not a precondition for love.

So what do we really mean by 'compatibility'? It is, after all, one of the leading terms in the modern vocabulary of love. We have to admit two points. On the one hand it is naive to neglect the destructive power of seriously divergent tastes, needs and interests. But on the other hand it is a mistake to infer from this that avoiding such conflict is the same as finding love. On reflection what emerges is this: there is no such thing as perfect compatibility. Therefore all loving relationships must accommodate some degree of incompatibility. Understanding how love can flourish in the face of some degree of incompatibility will, therefore, be one of the major questions we shall have to address.

A second striking feature of the myth which Plato assigns to Aristophanes is the claim that we have to go backwards to find love. The bisected half-beings who long for love have to find the 'other half' which they used to be attached to if they are to find love and be made whole. The person we can love, the thought goes, is one to whom we were connected in the past. Of course, amongst the few certainties in the discussion of love is the fact that we were not bisected in a previous stage of existence. But the Platonic myth aroused much interest in the twentieth century when it came to be interpreted as an allegory of a real split which occurs in every life. We were literally joined to someone before birth – we did experience symbiosis in the womb. Just as importantly, there is an experience of symbiosis in childhood – unless things go very seriously wrong.

When suckling goes well, the infant is in a significant way completed by the mother's breast and arms – and such completion is a poignant, and universally recognized, image of contentment. Indeed right through childhood the infant has a periodic sense, we might powerfully imagine, of complete contentment in the presence of a caring and attentive parent. These moments correspond to the prior state of the myth – only with a major revision. The person, or persons, with whom we were so connected are not themselves possible objects of romantic love. They institute, if they are loving, a template of what it is to be loved; but as adults we must find that recollected contentment with someone else, if we are to find it at all. The broad outlines of this view of the origins of love have become familiar through the work of Freud and Melanie Klein – although in their work many other more contentious claims are woven into this description of infancy.

It is this view of the origins of love in childhood which has sponsored a tragic conception of adult love. We are always seeking, in our adult loves, to return to a situation which cannot in fact be recreated. We try to find in our adult loves the complete security and ease which, from time to time, we experienced as children. But why can't we find this as adults? The Platonic myth, remember, posits a profound reciprocity: the person who completes me is, in turn, completed by me. This does not normally apply to the childhood model we are constructing. Although the adult may be delighted by the child this is, for the adult, usually just one strand within a much more complex existence. If things go well, the mother will have other concerns – other children perhaps, a career, domestic demands, a lover, friends. And, for the mother, a baby is a temporary item: a baby will grow up; a baby who didn't grow up would be a nightmare.

In other words, the loving parent creates a necessary and benign illusion; one which the child cannot see past. The illusion is that the baby is everything to the mother, just as the mother is – at good moments – everything to the child. There is a painting by Giovanni Bellini in the National Gallery in London which depicts the infant Christ sleeping in the lap of his mother, Mary. *The Madonna of the Meadows* gains its visual power from a crucial thought which it exemplifies. The infant is sleeping peacefully, the mother is lost in thought; in the background symbolic animals refer to the appalling death which this child will face as a man. We know what the mother is thinking: she is thinking – as all parents do – of the fact that her child will suffer and that there will be nothing she can do to avert it; that her child will die. This highly specific mother and child represent a universal theme. The child innocently reposes in the security and warmth of the mother's protection, while the mother – and the onlooker – knows the fragility and impermanence of this state.

It is this which explains why the attempt to return to the childhood template of love cannot succeed. No one can be everything to another adult – unless there is something very wrong with that person. No one can give an adult the kind of security a child feels, because to be an adult is to know that security is not permanent and is never a complete bulwark against suffering and loss. To try to recapture the condition of a loved child is an attempt to recreate a situation as seen from one side, not the situation as it really was. Yet if, as the theory posits, we cannot help but try to return, cannot help but model our adult vision of love upon the remains of childhood experience, then love would be a tragedy. There would be an ineliminable conflict between the core ideal of love and the reality of possible adult relationships. The thing we most want – on this view – is necessarily unattainable. We would be, as it were, psychologically geared for disappointment.

This pessimistic argument has some grip on the problems of adult love. There can be no doubt that some people do go in search of an impossible model of love. What they want love to be gets in the way of being loving adults. But as a general thesis, this claim is overstated. The flaw is not hard to see. One strand in the development of a vision of love is exaggerated and treated as if it were the only source of an adult view of love. If the desire for love were simply a disguised attempt to return to the condition of being loved as an infant, love between adults would be impossible. But while we should acknowledge that childhood plays a role in fashioning our, perhaps unconscious, models of love it is not plausible to insist that this is the only model we have.

The myth of original unity has had a powerful influence because of the way it suggests that we live with some kind of lack or inadequacy which we hope can be redeemed in love. Aristophanes beautifully evokes our longing to find the right person and the sense of fulfilment which may come from being with them; but he offers no explanation of what we need from the other person. What kind of insufficiency or incompleteness do we suffer, how can we account for the fact that we do, sometimes, feel like stray halves? What is it we lack? What is it we are searching for? One of the difficulties of using the mother–baby model to think about adult love is that while we know pretty well what babies need from their mothers it is much harder to pin down what it is adults need from each other. The baby longs for the mother's milk, physical warmth and comfortable arms. But what is it adults want from each other when it comes to love?

6

love as education

It falls to Socrates, Plato's mouthpiece in the *Symposium*, to take the discussion a step further. 'What do we find lovable?' Socrates asks as a way of trying to sharpen our sense of what it is we long for from the other. When we think about those we love, he suggests, we find in them admirable qualities. They are, perhaps, beautiful, sweet-natured, self-possessed or funny. We naturally say that we love them for these things. And to this Socrates adds a crucial point. We particularly relish in the other precisely the qualities that we lack ourselves. (It would be absurd, he says, to crave what you already possess.) We fancy, Socrates suggests, that in loving the other we can come, by some mysterious process, to possess those qualities. It is not a physical lack that drives us but a psychological one.

The desire of the lover, Socrates suggests, is like the desire of one who delights in learning and who loves knowledge. This is not the position of someone who is completely ignorant, but rather of one who already possesses some understanding: enough to feel the appeal of what lies ahead. So too with the love of the qualities we see in another. Those virtues call to us not because we lack them entirely but because they have not yet been fully brought forth in us. We feel, for example, that the wit of another will bring out our own qualities of mind, that their courage will strengthen our resolve, that their sweetness of manner will be the setting in which a more tender aspect of ourselves can emerge in safety. In short, we hope to become better and happier, and more truly ourselves, by being close to this other person. Their character, as we imagine it to be, seems to be the perfect setting for the development of our own qualities.

Taking the suggestion generously, Socrates has pointed to something of real importance. One of the questions that obsessed Greek writing on love was this: what does it take to be a successful lover? Conventional, and reasonable, answers tended to list the qualities the successful lover needs. It helps to be rich, powerful and clever. The first two enable you to give your beloved gifts and favours; cleverness helps you argue past any objections that might remain to your suit. But this list of positive attributes misses something crucial. If your loved one is really to matter to you, that person must possess something you don't have, must enable you to do something you can't do on your own. The capacity to win the regard of another depends on one's merits; the deep need to be close to someone else has a different origin entirely. If we were self-sufficient, love would be for us what the Greeks imagined it was for the Gods: an elegant, sometimes mischievous, amusement.

As the discourse develops Socrates argues that we undergo a serious disenchantment: we discover that however closely we embrace a beautiful, witty, serene person those qualities will not, of their own accord, become our own. To take possession of these good qualities we have to cultivate them in ourselves. It is not really other people we love, he continues, but the qualities we see in them. And gradually we progress from the love of individuals to the love of beauty and goodness in themselves; and it is through that more elevated love that we finally come to possess these things. This is the 'ladder of love' by which we rise from earthly, immediate affections to a love for and possession of abstract, universal virtues. Christian thinkers were to make much of this vision as a means of describing the soul's ascent towards the love of God. One attraction of this is the way it intimates that lesser loves are not a distraction from the final purpose of life but necessary stages on the way. Whether or not this speculative thesis charms us, we might feel that in the early moves, at any rate, Socrates has usefully deepened the original point that love originates in inadequacy. For Socrates can concur that it is lack that fuels love, but it is a lack of certain qualities that we find admirable and good in themselves.

However, in the spectacular suggestion of the ascent from the love of another person to the love of the abstract and immortal form of the Good, it is clear that Socrates is moving away from, rather than deeper into, an account of love as we know it. He is a reformer of human nature; he wants to describe what we should do, as he sees it, rather than account for what we actually do. Nevertheless, behind the grand narrative a more immediately relevant point is lurking. The worry Socrates has here is that the presence of the other won't quite do what we hope, it won't in itself bring forward the qualities we would like to find in ourselves. And, sometimes at least, this is painfully justified, for two reasons. One is that our problems are always tenacious. The loving presence of another may temporarily assuage our insecurity, self-doubt, low self-esteem, a tendency to be defensive, anxious about work, financial worries and the rest; yet ultimately these problems have to be resolved, if at all, by our own development. Another may be able to help in that process, but they cannot do it for us. This is the useful truth that lies behind Socrates' assertion that being in the presence of virtue turns out to be insufficient for the cultivation of virtue in ourselves.

The other problem is that, of course, the other is not perfect and their primary function in life cannot be to assist us in getting past our own shortcomings. They cannot be infinitely patient, able to subordinate their own needs indefinitely in order to assist us. Sometimes they will be tired, bored, depressed, irritated. The longing of love operates with the imagined ideal that, if only we can get close to the person we love and live in their presence, we will be cured of our inadequacies. This is a hope which is echoed in Aristophanes' story of being completed by our other half. But this longing is at best going to be partially realized. No other person can complete us in that way; this is something we have to do for ourselves, even if we are lucky enough to find another person who is helpful and supportive and whose character tends to bring out the best in us.

When Socrates says that we love another person for certain qualities they possess this can sound almost like a truism – too obvious to have much significance. But in fact there is a radical edge to the remark. By talking about lovable qualities Socrates seeks to introduce a degree of order into the apparently chaotic realm of preference. He suggests that what makes a person lovable isn't really mysterious. A sweet-natured person is more lovable than one who is bitter; generosity is more attractive than meanness, intelligence more appealing than stupidity. Of course, these terms are rather crude – to be really attractive, a sweet-natured person shouldn't be sweet-natured about everything. They need to be insistent, indignant or angry when such reactions are called for. Equally, generosity is not displayed by simply paying for everything; it is more admirable if someone knows when to be generous and when to hold back. In other words, it is quite comprehensible why certain qualities of personality and character are attractive and lovable. The ideally virtuous person – the person who has the loveliest qualities of mind and character – would be the most lovable person. And this seems right. If we think about our own experience of love we are likely to conclude that we have loved people for their good qualities and found their weaknesses and vices an obstacle to love. Love, in this way, is quite closely allied to admiration. According to this line of thought we can say fairly well in what respects someone is lovable and in what respects they are not.

This idea was popular in the ancient world but perhaps sounds strange today. One reason for this might be that the word 'virtue' has come to be associated largely with sexual restraint, whereas its deeper meaning is connected with excellence in any area of life. In fact the idea that people are loved for their virtues is alive and well, only the current version happens to operate with a narrow range of desirable excellencies: wealth, style, sexual prowess and reliability. The problem is not – as conservative critics might suggest – that these are irrelevant characteristics. The problem is that a list like this misses out many other attractive qualities which are important for the long term.

This insight suggests why love often doesn't work out very well: mostly we don't have all that many virtues or have them only to a limited extent; people in general are simply not terribly lovable. It also reminds us that, as individuals, we might not be very good at appreciating the lovableness of another person. Another's grace of mind will be lost on us if we have no capacity to listen or take an interest; their compassion will pass us by if we are self-righteous or brittle; we may not be able to take someone seriously unless they are conspicuously successful. If it is virtue that is lovable, we have to be perceptive and appreciative in order to love. It may require some subtle discernment to see past a surface liability and recognize an underlying good quality. It often takes time for a virtue to manifest itself. Someone who is rather opinionated might be entertaining company for a while, but gradually we long for touches of self-doubt and uncertainty. We come to see that it is finer to be uncertain when uncertainty is in order than to thrust on confidently when confidence is hardly warranted.

In the last chapter we looked at the strengths and weaknesses of the idea of compatibility. Now the educative role of love which Socrates talks of draws attention to another concept closely related to compatibility and also very much part of our modern vocabulary of love: complementarity. It would be hopeless

if the benefits in a relationship went always in one direction, if we saw the couple as composed of an educator
and a pupil. Yet surely it is obvious that this relation can
run in both directions: one person is strong in one area,
their partner in another. Each helps the other to become
a more rounded and better balanced person; each completes the other in that way. Further, the kind of education which Socrates points to is misleading – for an
interesting reason. Socrates has tried to pick out the
kind of knowledge which he considers most important
in life. As Plato's mouthpiece he asserts a highly unusual and highly intellectual vision of what we need to
know in order to thrive as individuals. Plato held that
abstract knowledge, knowledge of the forms, was the
only sure guide to the good life. But we can think of
loving partners educating each other in a rather different
way – not so much leading one another to an apprehension of 'the form of the good' as educating each other
emotionally.

What might this mean? The sustained kindly interest
of another person can, for example, ease a tendency to
excessive self-criticism. Or, the attention we devote to
the concerns and needs of another can take us out of
moods of self-pity and despondency. When things go
well, being close to another person corrects the biases of
one's own personality. These are themes to which we
shall return. For the present I merely want to record
such possibilities as a counter to the intellectual, Socratic
vision of what we may learn from another person. But I
want to retain the general insight which Socrates presents: what we learn with another person is part of what
we find lovable. It is not merely the other person, regarded

as separate, that inspires love. Benign power – good influence – can, if we are lucky, be part of what we find to love in our beloved.

recognition

As we have just seen, the Platonic account of love, transmitted via the persona of Socrates, stresses the developmental or educational aspect of love: we want to overcome our problems, we want to be better than we are. And without denying the significance of this as a factor in the longing for love, such a longing to be cured by another is clearly only a part of what may be going on. Another, and just as powerful, impulse is to be loved as we are. Few things in life are as delightful as feeling that another is delighted by us. The desire to please and to be liked is obviously deeply ingrained in human nature; without it we could hardly have contained our destructive capacities. But what do we want to be cherished for? Of course we often try to please others by doing what it is we think they want, or by being the sort of person of whom we imagine they will approve. But behind this there is a longing that others will delight in us just because of who we are.

When we think of ourselves, usually we do not think so much in terms of this or that character trait but of an imprecise and elusive individuality: what it is like to be me, to see the world through my eyes, with my kind of feelings, my individual spirit. Precisely because it is private, this 'inner-self' is not defined by achievements or knowledge or accomplishments but rather by the personal style of our approach to existence. We think back and say, 'It's the same me': I was that little person who used to lie on the bedroom floor half under the bed. It's not just that we remember doing or feeling something. It's that there's something about the way of feeling that is experienced as living on into the present. Perhaps we tend to think that what is kept quiet must be veiled because it is in some way shameful or pitiful; but the secret self I am interested in here probably stays secret for more interesting reasons. We are not very good at finding the right words to convey certain impressions. (Everyone knows what a cello sounds like, points out Wittgenstein, yet hardly anyone can describe it convincingly.) Also, we generally feel the need to protect an area of sensitivity from abrasion; mostly we have to encounter the world under the protection of a fairly thick skin. This private sense of oneself may be reclusive but not because there is something shameful in it.

Though no doubt an abuse of metaphysics, it is natural to think of this as a kind of private essence of personality. We sometimes feel that while another person knows about us, they don't really know who we are. Our inner character escapes them. This is a key source of the feeling of isolation that can sweep over us; the sense that we live surrounded by others but alone inside ourselves. We want another person to see and be delighted by just this essence, so that they say, 'It's you, just the way you are, that I love.' Not you with all your faults and occasionally rather horrible little ways. Instead, the essential you. Sometimes we playfully put this to the test: 'Would you still love me if I lost my looks, my money, my sense of humour? After all, I would still be the same me inside.' But this imaginative brinkmanship isn't really to the point. We don't suppose that a relationship could be sustained just on that slender basis. But within a more complex and diversely supported relationship we hope that this 'essence' will be recognized and that, along with many other things that might please our partners, it will be the object of a special regard. This is quite easy to see in the way parents love their children. While no parent ignores their child's accomplishments and achievements, it is clearly the child's personality, their own small way of being, that is the special object of fascination and charm.

Perhaps the most fundamental fact of human experience is that the experience of being oneself differs radically from the experience we have of others. We are inside our own thoughts and emotions; the thoughts and emotions of everyone else have to be gleaned, more or less accurately, by perception of what they do and say. To be lonely is to feel a distressing gulf between the character of one's own inner life and what seems to be the experience of others. Thus the paradigm of loneliness comes not in the absence of others but in the presence of other people to whom one's own way of thinking and feeling seems alien. It is with people who haven't a clue what you are on about, as you tentatively reveal your special pleasures, hopes or fears, that the burden of being alone is felt. The need to be loved is, amongst other things, the need to reverse this situation: the need to find someone who can say (often enough), 'I know how you feel, not just because you are telling me about it but because that's how I feel too.' It is this coincidence of feeling that we try to describe when we say that someone, a friend or a lover, understands us 'intuitively'. They don't need lengthy descriptions or explanations because they have, on the basis of their own internal experience, a grasp of what is at stake. From this point of view we can see why friendship is a species of love.

Sometimes when we meet another person we have an instinctive sense that we're going to get on well with them, that the possibilities of friendship are open. This is not only because we find that we can rub along comfortably with them, work amicably with them, find them interesting (although obviously these aspects are important); in that initial moment it's often the feeling that there is something about their mode of being, about the texture of their inner life, which seems familiar. There are convivial friendships based on congruence of interest or taste. And there are, more rarely, friendships based on a congruence of spirit. 'You seem to know,' the feeling goes, 'what it is like to look out at the world from behind my eyes, and not because I have told you.'

One of the central things we are looking for, as we look for love, is that this secret self should find a home in the eyes of another person, who will look upon this intimate aspect with pleasure. Indeed, a very specific sort of pleasure. What the phrase 'the apple of your eye' brings to mind is not just one pleasure among others, but a pleasure which is particularly relished – that in taking this pleasure I am enacting something which I find very special in my sense of myself. The longing for love is the longing that our sense of isolation will be pierced and that another will enter into the private areas of our existence in a tender and appreciative way.

Of course, if there is any truth in this as an account of what one longs to receive, there will also be some truth in the idea that it is this 'essential self' – as we see it – which we find lovable in another person. This is the corrective to the Socratic list of virtues which we considered in the previous chapter. It is when we discover, or suspect, some intimate correspondence between our own secret self and that of the other that we begin to move from liking to loving.

The word 'love' stands at the summit of our ethical vocabulary. Love is often presented as the most benign attitude we can have towards a person or thing. But there is a darker strain which needs to be recognized. In *The Outsider*, Albert Camus describes a man who is constantly followed by a little dog, his only companion. He is forever cursing, kicking and deriding this poor creature. Yet when it dies he is bereft – he 'loved' the dog. This is a model of one of the most frightening and paradoxical of states: a woman endlessly criticizes and upbraids her boyfriend – because she loves him; a man beats up his wife when he suspects her of being unfaithful – because he loves her so much. This attitude might be summed up as a statement: 'I hate you out of love for you.' The horror of isolation – of being alone with oneself – gives, perhaps, a clue to what is going on here. The abuser in such cases is profoundly attached to the victim. The attachment is a resort against isolation – thoughts, actions, feelings can be directed out onto the other person. The other person provides the necessary exit from oneself. But this would be lost if the other were simply to flee; their presence is needed and continually sought out. This is not simply hatred because it involves extreme possessiveness – and the feeling that the abuse is 'for the good of the other'.

Such terrible distortions of love are doubtless enacted episodically – and in a lesser degree – in all loves. They reveal, in horrible purity, the way in which the very needs which take us into love may play a role in the souring of love.

8

a creative eye

We have just considered a special kind of recognition which lovers find (or hope to find) in each other. But recognition has a more complex, more creative, aspect than has so far been mentioned.

Self-consciousness, Hegel once suggested, exists only in being acknowledged by another. This might well seem counter-intuitive at first: isn't it obvious that self-awareness is the very thing that is most obvious to us, how could we depend upon others for that? If we think about it, however, self-consciousness has two contrasting aspects. On the one hand, there is the immediate awareness of appetites, desires, affects and perceptions. This is shared by all conscious creatures. But self-consciousness, as we know it, also involves having a perspective upon our thoughts, desires and feelings. Sometimes this occurs in moral or epistemological terms: a desire may be deemed unacceptable, a thought may be doubted, a pleasure may be renounced. In this respect humans seem quite different from other animals. While very important, this insight only captures one part of the perspective we have upon our conscious states. Another part can be approached by analogy.

Imagine you have spent the morning wandering the

streets of an old French town, one you have never visited before. You see much that interests and pleases you. But it is only when, in the afternoon, you climb the church tower and look down on the streets that you see how the many things you noticed are related. As they occur, relationships between events do not announce themselves, any more than relationships between different parts of the town. It is only when you find another point of view that you see how they fit together. This is the second aspect of self-consciousness: the way we put together all that we are conscious of. We draw together and take an over-view of many things that we experience sequentially. To cash in the analogy: in self-consciousness we relate, and are aware that we relate, many different episodes of experience. A sedate dinner with an old friend may make one think back to a raucous evening of drunkenness many years ago and bring with it a sense of having changed and a series of thoughts about the nature of change. Self-consciousness stretches across time and holds together a continuous sense of oneself across the years.

But if this gives us a bigger image of what consciousness consists in, it perhaps doesn't yet shed much light on Hegel's strange insistence that self-consciousness depends on other people. To come nearer to an appreciation of that idea we may benefit from another analogy. Consider the way in which a child comes to see its own body. It is obvious that a baby is aware of its ears, limbs and so on; but it is only when it sees itself reflected in the mirror that it comes to see what it looks like. This is not just a matter of seeing its face, but of seeing the relations between the parts of its body, how they cohere. Of course, you don't need an actual looking-glass; children have come to see themselves through seeing other people, and come to internalize the structure of other bodies as their own. The child can see its arms, legs and so on, but something further occurs when it sees these as integral parts of a whole body. In other words, an important feature of self-awareness depends upon the 'mirroring' of ourselves in other people.

Something similar occurs with respect to the mind. There is really only one way of grasping the order of your limbs. But when it comes to putting experiences together the situation is more complex. There are many different ways in which we can order all the things that happen, many different ways in which we can regard experiences as significant or insignificant. You dream of a house on fire – what weight you give to this isn't preordained by the dream itself. You might see it as the product of indigestion, as a prediction, as an emanation of the unconscious. These ways of 'schematizing' or ordering experience are not made up by us as individuals but derive from the general culture we inhabit – they come, in other words, from other people.

In self-consciousness, we grasp (more or less accurately) our personality as a whole; we think of ourselves as being a particular kind of person. These 'perspectival' and 'holistic' aspects of self-consciousness are the mental equivalent of the child looking in the mirror. But in this case the 'mirror' is made of other people. It is how one appears in the eyes and minds of others that comes back as the material from which this crucial part of self-consciousness is constructed. So, the child comes to feel lovable when it sees that its parents see it as lovable. The parents' actions, tone of voice, way of looking, smiling, responding, become the reflective surface in which the child sees itself as lovable. Its own actions, gestures, feelings and words are taken up and given back by the parent. This complex kind of reflection, which transforms what it receives, is a crucial vehicle for the formation of self-consciousness; that is, for the child's view of itself.

Although we have been using the language of vision, this is slightly misleading. It is evident from the example of the child that it is not just the way another sees us but also how they respond, how they develop what we offer, how they sidestep obstacles, how they bring out what is interesting or valuable in what we do or say or feel, that is at stake. And this shows, too, the subtle difference between this kind of 'reflection' and flattery. The parent isn't saying to the child, simply, everything you do is perfect. Instead the parent is (as it were) repairing, editing, adjusting, retuning the material the child presents, so that it comes back to the child in a more integrated and valuable (and lovable) form.

In other words, there is a special lack of self-sufficiency which seems to be part of the structure of the human mind. Because in a sense we are too close to ourselves, we have difficulty in obtaining a perspective upon what we do and how we think. We need the interpretive attention of another to help us see ourselves in a more balanced way. Although 'to see ourselves as others see us' is a byword for humiliation, this is unduly pessimistic. Most people are just as given to excessive self-criticism and low self-esteem as they are (occasionally) to an exaggeration of their merits. So seeing ourselves reflected in another's eyes can, at least some of the time, be a pleasant experience. Only a deranged person goes around with a high opinion of their character and conduct; in order to be an interesting and attractive person we need to be fully alive to our failings. We need other people to take on the role of presenting back to us the more pleasant aspects of ourselves in an appreciative light. Of course there is a condition on this: the picture that comes back must make sense to us. To be extravagantly praised for something we really don't have any interest in is alienating: it is to feel that we are, in the eyes of this other person, someone quite different from who we take ourselves to be. Although entertaining in the short term it is, ultimately, wearying to be applauded for qualities you simply don't possess.

In looking for love, then – in romance, friendship, with our parents or children – we are looking for recognition of who we are: recognition which must somehow steer between praise and plausibility.

possession

So far, we have been exploring the idea of insufficiency primarily in terms of the loved one giving something to us, or doing something for us in an active way: improving us, providing recognition and benign interpretation. But there is perhaps also something more curious and passive that the lover seeks in the beloved. When St Augustine took up the theme of the lover's insufficiency – and this is the cornerstone of his thinking about love – he saw human beings as essentially desiring creatures and desire as a state of inadequacy and anxiety. No one, of course, is going to deny that humans are given over to desires, but the point of seeing this as an essential characteristic was to bring to attention a peculiar problem. The simple way of thinking about desire is this: you long for something, if you're lucky or skilful or clever you take possession of it. You are happy. But unfortunately this is not quite how things work out. The reason, according to Augustine, is that as soon as you have what you desired you suddenly find that getting it has only served to stimulate new and unforeseen wants. Desire, then, is organic: it grows. The more you feed it, the more you give it what it wants, the bigger and stronger it gets. And of course, the stronger our cravings, the less we feel satisfied. Augustine presents, in rather apocalyptic terms, a phenomenon which, in more modest versions, is not unfamiliar. Looking round your sitting-room you may wish you could afford a fine overmantel mirror, you covet a chrome-plated standard lamp. But in comparison with what you accepted as a student you are now living in comparative luxury. So there is something in the nature of desire itself, its capacity to generate new wants no matter what we have, which precludes fulfilment. In St Augustine's eyes, one of the things we long for is relief from the apparently futile cycle of desire – a theme echoed 1,500 years later by Schopenhauer. But this longing is essentially a longing for love. Why?

Love, Augustine thought, allows for a special kind of possession that stills our desires. When we lovingly possess another person, their presence puts us completely at ease and brings relief from desires. For the other person enters into our life in a deep way and engages with the source of our inadequacy, and hence with the mainspring of our demands on the world. After all, why do we want the mirror or the lamp; why do we long for promotion or extra income? Of course there are multiple answers: we want to be more comfortable, we want prestige, we want our abilities to be rewarded and recognized; we want our homes to look charming and elegant. But still, why do we want these things? What do we think they will bring us? Even if we are not entirely convinced by Augustine, it is at least worth considering his suggestion that our longing for all these things is an obscure and indirect way of seeking that which love can bring us directly. For when we securely possess (love and are loved by) another, doesn't our perspective change?

This shift in perspective needn't be interpreted in the extreme form it has sometimes taken: you can live in a hovel, eat nothing but bread and water and be blissfully happy if only you have your loved one with you. ('The tiniest hut is large enough for true lovers,' writes Schiller in this vein.) But this is to caricature, by driving to excess, an otherwise interesting point. It is obvious that one can have a much better time in a cheap restaurant if you go there with someone you are deeply drawn to and who returns your feelings than you can in a gourmet palace with an awkward and edgy partner. But this doesn't entail that it wouldn't be nice to go there with your beloved.

Augustine overstates his case by suggesting that if we found what we were really looking for (love) our desires for other things would melt away. Perhaps a more plausible version is this. When we haven't got what we are looking for, our desires take on a special urgency and fervour. We feel we simply can't do without the mirror, the lamp, the glamorous restaurant. If we have love we may still enjoy these things, but possessing them plays a relatively less significant role in our lives.

By stating so clearly what we might like love to be (the solution to all our problems, what we really want in life, what everything else is a substitute for), St Augustine, perhaps unwittingly, lays down the gauntlet to a challenger. Can love really be as important as this? Does it really make such a difference as he supposes? Isn't this an idealization of love – a dream of life rather than a description of emotional reality? The answer, I think, is both yes and no. Perhaps Augustine is right if he is thinking of how love may seem from time to time. There are great moments of passion when we are faced with stark visions of love. When you think your baby might die in childbirth, who would not offer (could such an offer be taken up) to give up everything, to start again from nowhere, if only this would guarantee the baby's life? There is a radical alteration of perspective; for a moment we see existence in Augustinian eyes. All is vanity except our passionate love for this desperate creature. But who can live continually at this pitch?

One major concern which Augustine articulates is the way in which love involves a reorientation of our concerns. We are in the habit of being immensely preoccupied by what immediately concerns our own well-being. We are strongly attracted to comfort, prestige, money, applause. Yet none of these things, Augustine argues, can in the end bring us happiness. The reason, as we have seen, is that he is impressed by the inflationary aspect of such desires. We keep on wanting more comfort, more money, more power, more sex. Hence we always feel unsatisfied. It is only when we move outside this habitual sphere of self-seeking and start to love what lies outside of us (God, our neighbour) that we are released from the cycle of ever-increasing demands. Even if we do not accept the dramatic antithesis with which Augustine works, we can still be impressed by the basic suggestion. Which is this: caring for something, or someone, other than oneself can be immensely liberating.

The alteration in perspective comes to this: in comparison with the satisfaction we can find in true love (for Augustine, the love of God) everything else comes to look unimportant. This is closely related to the view Shakespeare elaborates in one of his best-known sonnets:

> When, in disgrace with fortune and men's eyes,
> I all alone beweep my outcast state,
> And trouble deaf heaven with my bootless cries,
> And look upon myself and curse my fate,
> Wishing me like to one more rich in hope,
> Featured like him, like him with friends possessed,
> Desiring this man's art, and that man's scope,
> With what I most enjoy contented least;
> Yet in these thoughts myself almost despising,
> Haply I think on thee, and then my state,
> Like to the lark at break of day arising
> From sullen earth, sings hymns at heaven's gate;
>> For thy sweet love remembered such wealth brings
>> That then I scorn to change my state with kings.

Shakespeare leaves it to the imagination of the reader (or recipient) of the sonnet to locate the underlying explanation: there is something about loving another person – and being loved in return – which outweighs the other goods he lists: good looks, friendship, ability, the world's praise. But he doesn't tell us what it is about love that makes it count for so much. He just assumes that we will recognize that this is how things are.

Augustine, by contrast, does try to flesh out an explanation. He believes that the soul is so constituted that we crave complete security and permanence. But we cannot attain these things through the pursuit of the goods of this world. However, they are offered by God. God, in other words, is the solution of the problem of existence. All the other things we crave are false responses to these most basic concerns.

Augustine presents us with a stark opposition: either

we devote ourselves wholly to love, love which is inherently selfless, or we suffer endless disappointment and insecurity. This is to make a bold supposition about a universal psychology. One of the most attractive features about Augustine as a writer and thinker is the attention he pays to his own experience. In his famous *Confessions* he traces the various stages in his life in which he sought contentment and failed to find it; it was only in middle age, when he became a Christian and devoted himself to the love of a personal God, that his discontent was relieved and he felt satisfied. This is an impressive individual story but it seems clear that Augustine was a remarkable individual, rather than – as he thinks – a representative specimen. It is true that we are all prone to insecurity and restlessness; but probably only a few people are as hard to satisfy as Augustine. For many people a successful career, or an attractive home, or pleasant friends are a tremendous and lasting source of satisfaction. Augustine longed to know the truth and was ruthless in his interrogation of all candidates for this high distinction. Most people are not like this and are not troubled if they are unable to come to an absolutely secure point of rest.

If we accept that there is a spectrum of need, then we should accept that the strenuous vision of love which Augustine advocates – love as the unique and complete solution to the problem of existence – is an exaggeration. Love plays an important part in reorienting us away from vain pursuits, but it is a mistake to think that love is the only pursuit which can bring real satisfaction. Indeed the irony is that the more we invest in love, the harder it can be to love successfully. To love another person often requires that we have further and independent sources of satisfaction and security in our lives. Shakespeare wonderfully brings this in from the start, with a single contextualizing word: 'When'. Love is not the only thing that matters in life, but when those other things let us down then love is consoling. But we could project a mirroring sonnet which reminds us that when love is not going well, art, friends and career can be consoling sources of security and happiness.

Of course, possession is not just one-way. The ideal of love is mutual possession: my beloved is mine and I am his, or hers.

> Now sleeps the crimson petal, now the white;
> Nor waves the cypress in the palace walk;
> Nor winks the gold fin in the porphyry font:
> The fire-fly wakens: waken thou with me.
>
> Now droops the milkwhite peacock like a ghost,
> And like a ghost she glimmers on to me.
>
> Now lies the earth all Danaë to the stars,
> And all thy heart lies open unto me.
>
> Now slides the silent meteor on, and leaves
> A shining furrow, as thy thoughts in me.
>
> Now folds the lily all her sweetness up,
> And slips into the bosom of the lake:
> So fold thyself, my dearest, thou, and slip
> Into my bosom and be lost in me.

Tennyson's words beautifully evince a sense of complete mutual possession and closeness. Your thoughts trace a shining furrow in my mind; I am open to you and you are open to me. This is the reciprocity which occurs when love meets with love. The poem also makes us alert to the temporary nature of such a union. There are privileged times when nothing comes between the lovers; there is a quiet harmony, a completeness in their mutual existence. But this is privileged against a background of more awkward times. Such moments require that both share a quiescent, tender mood. The first eight lines of the poem elaborate, and make us feel, this mood of attentive repose. The contemplative, concentrated feelings of the lover are communicated by the description of a resonant scene – the beauty of the garden and the night.

It often takes nothing more than the ordinary press of existence to impede this delicacy of feeling. This is why lovers have an affinity with all the things which help promote and sustain mutual inwardness: wine, open fires, candle-light, rain; whatever creates the temporary illusion of their own special, enclosed world, separated from the rest of life – all of which, for a while, seems shadowy and distant. And in such benign conditions they can feel that they are what they never really can be: everything, one to the other.

There is a story of the last two members of the United Kingdom Communist Party, a husband and wife, who (doubtless) believed themselves, in the whole world, the only two who possessed the true way of seeing the world. They looked out from their own superior and correct point of vantage on a world of confusion, wickedness and error. Whatever the folly of their convictions, they are (or were, until in a consummate act of heroic loneliness the man expelled the woman for doctrinal impurity) a poignant – though exaggerated – image of all happy couples. For all happy couples possess their own private ideology, their special way of looking at the world which they share and which they quietly regard as superior to all others.

All lovers create and need to create little signs and symbols of their sequestered state, of their pleasant distance from everyone else. It is also why home – our home – is the lover's natural symbol. This is common to all kinds of love: a couple of friends over dinner mutually promote a slight condescension, a touch of pity, for all others.

We have been considering the roots of love in human nature: the things about us which make us seek out a special kind of relationship with another person. The reality of these needs does not entail that they are explicitly recognized by one who has them. It is a well-founded axiom of the mind that the needs and desires which drive us may be present to us only in an obscure, veiled or distorted fashion. Think of the young child who is bored but can only articulate his distress by saying, 'I hate my toys, I hate you, daddy.' The parent recognizes the distress but discounts (as the child cannot) its distorted statement. The child is, naturally, unable to fathom what it is distressed about and latches on to the most conspicuous things in its world and blames them. And, perhaps, as we grow up, we get only marginally better at putting a finger on what it is that we lack, on what it is that distresses or excites us.

The idea that a longing may be veiled carries an important consequence. It is not just that we may find it hard to identify what we are looking for; there can also be a powerful motive for suppressing our longing for love. The whole thrust of this chapter has been to investigate forms of inadequacy and lack of self-sufficiency, and to see these as propelling us into love. But, of course, it can be disturbing, even terrifying, to admit such insufficiency to ourselves. 'Why do I need another person? Because I cannot be happy on my own?' For some people at least, this is too painful an admission. We sometimes avoid our need for love because it casts us in a vulnerable role. King Lear's high-handed, unloving attitude to Cordelia at the start of the play is the counterpart of his own intense fear of dependency and weakness. At the moment when he cedes power he must do everything he can to convince himself that he is still strong. And one way he does this is to dismiss from his sight the person who most vividly awakens in him the sense of his need for another – his youngest daughter. He cannot afford to love. More accurately, he has to attack the person who evokes his love, and he seeks to crush the tenderness and vulnerability in himself which respond to that call.

It is impossible to be comprehensive in listing the factors which combine to generate a need for love. But even an incomplete account of the roots of love can achieve three things. Firstly, it can suggest how deep the need for love goes in us. Secondly, it indicates how hard it sometimes is for us to recognize what it is we are looking for (which will have major implications for our sense of who might help us satisfy those longings). And lastly, it suggests how hard it is going to be for someone else to satisfy those needs. The future difficulties of love are already implicit in its origins.

10

imagination

When we fall in love, a massive effect is worked by an apparently slight cause. You see *her* walking down the street and you turn weak at the knees. *He* smiled in a sweet way when you waved; you are delirious for the rest of the day. Without imagination there would be no such thing as love. If we are to understand why sight or thought of a particular person should arouse such a response we need to think about the focus and elaboration of that person in our minds. And, in fact, this task of reflection is undertaken in – for all its faults – the single most insightful book on the role of imagination in love. This is Stendhal's *Love*, a work which grew out of his intense but unreciprocated attachment to a certain Mathilde Dembowski, whom he met in his mid-thirties when he was living in Milan.

The central way in which Stendhal describes the role of imagination is through a technical term which he introduces: crystallization. The inspiration for this term came from his observation of a natural phenomenon. A bare twig, he reports, is left in a disused salt mine in Salzburg. A few months later it is pulled out, now entirely encrusted with salt crystals. 'The smallest twig, no bigger than a tom-tit's claw, is studded with a galaxy of scintillating diamonds.' And the original twig is no longer recognizable. Stendhal makes this physical process serve as an analogy for a psychological one: imagination transfigures the image of the loved one. The process of falling and remaining in love is, Stendhal wants to persuade us, a process of crystallization. How does it work?

Suppose you meet someone you find fairly attractive; you might go on to think how nice it would be to kiss them, to hold their hand, to sit on the sofa and talk intimately, and if you have some hope that this might be possible, the process of falling in love can start. Left alone, the embryonic lover will think over the appeal of the about-to-be-loved one. Imagination comes into play as the image of the 'fairly attractive person' is encrusted with a range of charms. Perhaps you fancy lying in an orchard looking up at the sky through the branches. In imagination you now consider how additionally pleasant it would be to be there with your new acquaintance. The image of that person takes on a new feature: in addition to what you have seen of them they are endowed with a further charm, you imagine them as the sort of person who would share your feelings for the orchard and the sky. The beloved becomes a sensitive and relaxed being in your mind, whatever their real disposition.

Or you hear, for example, that a friend has broken his arm and will have to be nursed for weeks. 'Wouldn't it be wonderful,' you think, 'to be looked after by the one you love! A broken arm would be heaven.' Your friend's injury seems to provide you with evidence of the angelic kindness of your beloved. Prosaically stated, this is what is going on: an event makes a quality seem attractive – an injury shows the appeal of careful attention. In an atmosphere charged with recognition of that attractive quality the image of the other becomes encrusted with it, just as the crystals in the air of the salt mine attach themselves to the twig suspended down there. Left long enough in such a charged atmosphere the image of the beloved becomes successively covered with thoughts of this kind, until it would hardly be recognized as an image of them by a neutral observer.

But this is only the beginning. Suppose now, as is highly probable, you meet with 'some coolness or slight rebuff' on the part of the person with whom you are now falling in love. Whatever the original hopes, doubt gains a place in your feelings. Perhaps the other is indifferent; perhaps the initial hopes were misplaced? Given how deeply desirable that person has come to seem (loaded as they are with the fruits of imagination) this fear is exceedingly painful. You are now impelled to pore over every scrap of evidence to see whether it can be given a more hopeful interpretation. 'Perhaps,' you reflect, 'the indifference I observe is the result of wanting to keep passion in check; it indicates not lack of interest but, on the contrary, an enthusiasm which is so strong that it has disturbed the composure of my beloved.' Or perhaps you overheard a disparaging remark from the lips of the one you love. But isn't it possible that they are simply trying to conceal from others their passionate attachment? In which case the indifference and the disparagement become, under the transforming power of imagination, evidence of a positive attitude towards you. Then of course the doubt comes back in a new form, only to be opposed once again by another subtlety of interpretation. This is what Stendhal thinks of as the 'second crystallization' and it is at this stage, he believes, that love becomes fixed. Once we are in the habit of oscillating between fear and hope and subjecting every bit of evidence to elaborate consideration, our inner life becomes indissolubly linked to the other. We cannot tear ourselves free. This is love.

A crucial aspect of Stendhal's account is his insistence that such experience is far from universal. It presupposes the kind of person whose imagination is given free reign, who is not in the habit of weighing evidence dispassionately. People who in their ordinary course of business try always to see things as they are, Stendhal argues, are therefore less susceptible to love. He supposes that the habit of thought acquired in business seeps into their entire way of thinking. His enthusiasm for neat classification leads him, for once, to miss an interesting point: that, on the contrary, it is often the mind most cooped up by boring routine which explodes into romantic activity.

The function of imagination in developing passion doesn't only work in connection with love, of course, but also with its apparent opposite – hatred. The familiar crisis of a relationship comes when some small thing the other does gets massively on one's nerves. To an outsider this can seem like an amazing lapse of one's sense of proportion. 'Why does it matter to you so much that she always goes into the kitchen to give the work surfaces one last wipe before coming to bed?' 'Surely it isn't a big deal that he habitually leaves the cap off the toothpaste?' Regarded in an austerely rational light the objection is well founded. It only takes a moment to put the cap on; she'll come to bed in three minutes. But we experience things in quite a different way. When we see the cap off again we see – by the power of imagination – a symbol of a way of life. It is a general tendency exemplified in a single instance. The delay means an indifference to desire, an inability to feel overcome by passion; the cap stands for carelessness in general, indifference to the proper way of doing things. This is exactly the same mechanism (though working in an opposite cause) which operates when we fall in love. We do not, as it happens, use the phrase 'falling in hate', but the process is real nevertheless.

Stendhal, of course, is preoccupied with romantic love and with its initial stages. Precisely the failure to establish any substantial mutual relationship with Mathilde is reflected in the obsessive, but highly revealing, attention he pays to falling in love: the stage at which, luckily for us, his experience got stuck. But the strength of his analysis is borne out by the easy application it finds in relation to other cases of love. Doesn't a parent dwell endlessly on the charms of their child; doesn't the patriot find in every feature of the native landscape yet another reason to love his country? The child and the land become encrusted in this process of loving attention so that they become almost unrecognizable to others. We saw, in the discussion of longing, how the desire for love emerges from a group of deep-set psychological needs. Stendhal helps us to trace one of the major ways in which, through imagination, we build up an image of another person as fitting our character. In Stendhal's eye, through the process of crystallization, another person is perceived as perfectly fitting the template of our needs.

infatuation

The very idea of infatuation implies an external, or historical, perspective. When you are infatuated, by definition you cannot know that this is what you are. Like being deceived, or having a mistaken conviction, it must seem, to one who suffers it, just like the real thing. It is only to another person (or to yourself at a later date) that your passion is judged 'just an infatuation'. The fact of infatuation, as a kind of shadow form of love, gives rise to a problem. For we want to say that there is a difference – a difference that is in play even as the passions occur – between infatuation and real love. Only whatever it is that constitutes this difference is, subjectively, unavailable while the passion occurs. So what is the difference? Can we pick up an insight into real love by seeing what is missing in infatuation?

One of the great literary studies of infatuation comes in Turgenev's late novel *Spring Torrents*. The novel tells the story of an encounter between a young Russian nobleman, Sanin, who is passing through Germany on his way home from Italy, and a beautiful Italian girl, Gemma, whose mother runs a café in Frankfurt. Trying to order a glass of lemonade, Sanin gets drawn into the family; distracted by Gemma's ivory skin and wavy hair he misses the coach and decides to spend a few more days around Gemma, only to find that she is engaged to be married. Over the next few days, Sanin is enchanted by Gemma and by 'the black depths of her eyes suffused with shadows and yet luminous at the same time'. He senses that she doesn't really care for her fiancé, a successful – but unpoetic – shopkeeper called Kleuber. On a pleasure trip Gemma is addressed rudely by some officers; Kleuber wisely ignores the incident but Sanin, imagining he is defending her honour, issues a challenge, fights a duel and survives. Gemma is electrified by this gesture and Kleuber is dismissed. Sanin and Gemma exchange ecstatic love letters; she agrees to marry him; he decides to sell his Russian estates and move to Frankfurt. Sanin feels overwhelmed by love:

He was no longer debating anything inwardly, no longer reflecting, calculating, looking ahead. He had left the past entirely behind him, he had plunged headlong into a mighty flood. Never mind what grief it might bring, never a thought for where the flood would carry him or indeed for the possibility that it would dash him to pieces. Here were mighty waves which could not be restrained.

Everything seems to be settled. Sanin hears that a potential purchaser for his property – a very wealthy young married Russian woman, Maria Nikolaevna – is in the district. He sets off 'for two days at most' to settle the business. However, he is immediately seduced by her powerful personality and her voracious sexuality. Sanin abandons Gemma and sets off for Paris with Maria Nikolaevna and her tame husband.

The rapid, melodramatic finish Turgenev provides for Sanin's affair with Gemma merely exaggerates the central point: there was something lacking in that passion, even though Sanin was enraptured. Can we really imagine the dandyish Sanin selling up in Russia and spending the rest of his days managing the family café and living on happy terms with Gemma's slightly hysterical mother? This was not a realistic plan for his life, just a delightful play; the imagined future was too thin, too insubstantial.

The idea of infatuation shows us the downside of imagination. Sanin, in a sense, is highly imaginative; he is carried away not by the real possibilities of a life with Gemma, not even by the girl as she really is, but by a romantic fiction which he has elaborated around her and her family. The fantasy he elaborates is attractive, the problem is that it does not correspond with the reality of his personality and needs. His rapid seduction by Maria Nikolaevna is used, I think, to show us a more profound and disturbing current in Sanin's character, a current which his fantasy about Gemma not only omits but positively avoids. Sanin, like Turgenev himself (and the writer made no secret of the autobiographical aspect of the novel), is a man profoundly troubled by freedom, who longs, in fact, to have freedom taken from him. But this is hardly a longing which anyone would gladly recognize. The infatuation with Gemma and the absurd duel which Sanin fights – benefiting no one and risking his own life – concoct a fantasy of himself as a man of action, a potential paterfamilias, a man of business (running the café). It's not just that these are pleasant thoughts, they are thoughts which run counter to his real personality. Sanin's infatuation is fuelled not only by

Gemma's charm (which is real) but also by the need to evade more disturbing thoughts about what kind of relationship might actually suit him. For Sanin, what he wants and what suits him do not neatly coincide.

Turgenev has shown us a crucial feature of infatuation – that it can be driven not just by a mistake about the other person (thinking they are nicer than they really are) but by a mistake about oneself (wanting to be other than one is). Perhaps 'mistake' is the wrong term here. It's not so much that Sanin makes an intellectual error; it is, rather, that he is deeply drawn to an appealing vision of himself – but one which deliberately does not admit his own weaknesses and fears. In infatuation, we use another person as a prop in a fantasy about ourselves.

This view of infatuation – attraction to what we want, not to what we need – suggests a profound and disturbing thesis about how love sometimes goes. Deep love might attach us to someone who in the end is highly suitable but who doesn't, superficially, offer us what we want. Take the example of a man with a tendency to drink too much, to be profligate. It may be that – in some obscure way – he recognizes that a woman who will not go along with these desires will actually be the right sort of person to have a long-term relationship with. But for years he may berate her for being strait-laced and puritanical, may spend his evenings increasingly wondering why he ever got together with her. Only to come to see, eventually, that the last thing he needed was someone who would turn round and say, 'Let's have another bottle – why not make it two?' Or who giggled when she found bank statements unopened in the bin. This is an extreme case but it serves, perhaps, to remind us that in love – considered as a long-term relationship – the stakes are high and our immediate inclinations, our present wants, may provide a very poor guide when it comes to identifying a possible partner. Love can sometimes rise up like a desperate cry from a neglected part of oneself which takes a long view but which is submerged by the presence of strident wants.

A further clue to what is going on can be found, I think, if we examine an instance of infatuation which occurs outside romantic love. Imagine someone who has never had a child or any long-term responsibility for children who says, 'I long to have children, I know how much I would love them, how fulfilled I would be walking around with a baby in a sling and another in a push-chair.' This is sincere and well meant. But it sounds like a lightweight promise. It speaks from a lack of experience. It doesn't take into account any real grasp of what it might be like to try to get a recalcitrant three-year-old into a car seat while your one-year-old is crying because the rain is dripping onto her face. You are doing this in a hurry so you can get them to the nursery in time. You're exhausted because the older one climbed out of bed three times last night and the younger one was crying because of an ear infection. Perhaps you will remain calm and loving, but can you promise this in advance? What an example like this indicates is that the weight a person's words have depends on the extent to which they have relevant experience in their sights. The would-be-ever-loving parent hasn't earned the right to make substantial claims about their future behaviour. But, of course, it doesn't seem to the speaker that a wild promise is being made; the assertion feels secure and well founded. Such a person imagines that it is the quality of current feeling that matters; in fact, current feeling is no guide to behaviour under multiple strains and stresses. What infatuation does is to consecrate the present feeling (how nice it would be to live with X/to have a baby) and protect it from serious investigation. Imagination paints a charming view of the future, conveniently adapted to the demands of our current emotion.

Infatuation is anticipatory – it looks towards fulfilment and a blissful future. But the character of the anticipation is determined by our hopes rather than by understanding. We can see that the problem of infatuation is not so much that the would-be lover is too imaginative, but that they are imaginative in one direction – only when it comes to thinking how nice everything could be. When suffering from the unwanted attentions of an infatuated admirer, the best thing might be to have a fling with them and then take them shopping for groceries and washing-up liquid. If infatuation is based on fantasy, the cure is a generous serving of banality.

The would-be lover or parent is sincere; their passions are real to them. Sincerity, like zeal and courage, is what is sometimes called an 'executive' virtue. That is, it increases the effectiveness of whatever it is one sets out to do. But one can be zealous in an absurd cause, courageous in pursuit of a mean goal – in which case the efficiency only increases the problem. Sincerity is only as good as what we are sincere about. One of the distinctive excesses of romantic psychology (a psychology which persists) is the overestimation of the value of sincerity. Not because it is, somehow, good to be insincere; that isn't the point. The point is that an excessive investment in sincerity makes us forget that there are other things which matter too – that everything depends upon what one is being sincere about. We are so aware of how things go wrong when people are insincere that we forget that sincerity is manner, not substance. This is among the crueller ironies of existence.

In a way what goes wrong with someone who becomes infatuated – and thinks it is love – is that they are operating with an insufficient range of emotional categories. Perhaps when we are so eagerly searching for the profundity and security of reciprocal love we can hardly stop ourselves promoting each attachment to the highest grade. ('I was desperate for a deep relationship, and X charmed me in certain ways.') The better option – but it is one which requires a degree of maturity – is to align infatuation with friendship, not with romantic love.

12

blind cupid

In the opening chapters of this book we considered some of the psychological needs which draw us out of a self-contained existence and propel us into a longing for things which only other people can give us. In later chapters, we turned to the distinctive way in which, as we fall in love, those longings become focused on another person – primarily through the work of imagination. I want now to widen the discussion and take into consideration something obvious which we have not yet considered in any detail: love is a passion – an emotion – and falling in love is one of the most potent and dramatic emotional experiences we ever have.

In Cupid, the god whose arrows make us fall in love, the ancient world personified its sense of how people fall in love. Cupid, sometimes called Eros (the names deriving from 'desire' in Latin and Greek), is an external agent who, without consulting us, makes us long passionately to possess and be close to some particular other person. Falling in love is caused by something outside us and beyond our control. In the *Amores*, Book I, Ovid refers to himself repeatedly as Cupid's 'victim', his 'prisoner' and 'captive'. This dramatizes the idea that it is not up to us whether or not we fall in love, nor with whom;

it happens, whether or not it corresponds to our wishes.

To this extent Ovid is right: we do not first of all pick out, on reasonable grounds, someone with whom it would make sense to have a relationship and then, as a consequence of our reasonable choice, fall in love. And sometimes there does appear to be a species of randomness at work. You might fall in love with someone who would never be a satisfying partner, who is (perhaps) unavailable, indifferent to you, or just in temper, taste and mode of life incompatible with you. Or it may be that you meet someone who seems, to a rational observer, to be very well suited to a long-term relationship; yet you don't get fired up, love doesn't ignite.

In the later *Metamorphoses*, Ovid attributes to Cupid the further power of preventing someone from feeling love. In the famous story of Daphne and Apollo, the god has been struck by one of Cupid's shining golden arrows and falls passionately in love with Daphne. However, the girl flees the entreaties of the god; relentlessly pursued she implores her father, a river god, to save her and by his power she is transformed into a laurel tree. Even in her leafy state Apollo's passion is undimmed and the laurel becomes sacred to him. Why did she resist the charms of the beautiful, magnificent god, the ideal of the desirable man? But Cupid had pierced her with a blunt, lead-tipped arrow, the kind which puts love to flight. (Have you not felt that the other must return your love were it not for some unaccountable, pointless quirk of resistance?)

This powerful image of the irrationality of love – or the avoidance of love – was deepened by imagining Cupid as a youth, even as a boy, by nature mischievous and irresponsible, moved at times by spite or vengeance. The allegory of Cupid expresses the idea that we do not choose our lovers out of understanding but in accordance with an alien logic which makes no reference to the good or happiness of the two parties. If we relish the image of Cupid, and continue to employ him as a reference, it is because he externalizes a process which we recognize. ('Why has she fallen for *him*? It's as if some malevolent, external force is driving her to certain misery.') An uncoupling of passionate intensity, or blank indifference, from the reasonable estimate of the suitability of the other person really does seem to occur. We feel passive and powerless in the face of something that compels us to hopeless hope, or which thwarts the most well-grounded hope, for apparently no reason. In other words, in at least some cases the image of Cupid as mischievous seems apt. This is not to say that, in general, people fall in love at random. That would certainly be false – usually, the 'object choice' may seem at first quite plausible. The image of Cupid makes most sense when we think of cases of love in which the partners seem in some important way ill-matched, unable to bring each other any very obvious satisfaction. And yet the attachment, the passion, persists – on one side at least.

To say that a passion is irrational may be to say a number of quite different things, more or less plausible, which we can differentiate by carefully untangling the various implications of the term 'irrational'. Hunger, for example, is irrational: we don't feel hungry because it makes sense for us to do so. We might be faced with a delicious dish and simply not feel any appetite; we might become famished just at a moment when we are extremely busy and have no access to a sandwich. We may eat more or less than is good for us. Hunger isn't prompted or suppressed by reason. But this doesn't mean that how we act when hungry is also irrational. On the contrary we are, generally, rather good at controlling the impulse to eat and at selecting the sorts of things which taste nice and are reasonably nourishing. Eating is usually amenable to reason. So too with love: relationships are partly governed by forces within us of which we are not much aware. Hence, their consequences appear like the workings of an external agent. Cupid is the name of whatever it is in us which, without our consent or recognition, provokes the intense longing for attachment which we call falling in love. We do not choose who to fall in love with, and do not have control over the waxing and waning of ardour, because these forces are not directly subject to reason or the will.

Taken in this limited sense, the blindness (or irrationality) of Cupid would be less disturbing if we thought that, whatever the origins of love as a passion, we could remain in reasonable control of our actions. We might be struck by a yearning for a useless partner but we wouldn't, just because of that, have to act on the yearning or be unduly troubled by it. In other words, the fear of love as irrational is not simply the fear that love is in its genesis irrational, but that it is not amenable to reason once it is up and running. Again, Ovid puts this dramatically. Describing Apollo's passion for Daphne, he writes: 'As the light stubble blazes up in a harvested field, or as the hedge is set alight, if a traveller chance to kindle a fire too close, or leaves one smouldering when he goes off at day-break, so the god was all on fire, his whole heart was aflame.' Passion, the thought goes, takes over the mind; like fire it spreads to whatever flammable material is close by. The consuming passion of love disarms reason, it blinds us to good sense and rational action. We are besotted and can no longer judge whether our passion is in accordance with an intelligent course of action or not. We lose the power to weigh up the merits of the beloved. Love, in this pessimistic vision, is like a hunger which is so engulfing and intense that we become its slaves. The golden or leaden arrows of Cupid transmit a bulimia or anorexia of love which overruns the individual's capacity to act or think reasonably in the face of their passion.

This will always be how certain instances of passionate love seem to detached observers. What about the friend who tried to throw himself out of the car on the motorway when his – not especially nice – girlfriend called it a day? Why couldn't Werther, an attractive, intelligent, well-off young man, just go and find himself another nice young woman? Charlotte was lovely, certainly, but he didn't need to shoot himself just because she turned him down.

The irrationality becomes apparent – love appearing contrary to, rather than merely distinct from, reason – in such cases because the agent goes directly against his own well-being. The lover seems too desperate, too attached to a particular object for his own good. It is as if the fire of love has burned away any other resources he may have for finding a more helpful perspective on his passion. The 'folly' of love is evident when the lover has no means of detaching himself from the object, when he loses the power of giving up and simply feeling sad and hopeless for a while with regard to that attachment, rather than despairing of the possibility of happiness in general.

Someone who is famished might be tempted to eat something which would be rejected by anyone else. Anyone, that is, who was not too hungry or who had a confident belief that nourishment might soon come in a more palatable form. But the forces which make us long for another person to love (the forces we have examined in earlier chapters) – loneliness, the need to be close to another, to be needed by someone, the need for warmth and tenderness – can be so great that we behave as if we were starving. We are so desperate that we can't afford to be discriminating – whatever is available looks appealing to us. We fasten upon whatever, whoever, comes along. Desperation overrides discrimination. We can't withdraw when things go badly wrong; we can't be patient and wait for a more suitable person to come along.

By an ordinary logic we can see that falling in love with someone who makes us unhappy – and who can be recognized by others as an unsuitable partner in life – is irrational. It goes directly against our own chances of a happy life. However, it may be the case that such an unfortunate 'object choice' is in fact dictated by a powerful internal but unconscious process. This view was brilliantly argued for in the late 1940s by an American psychoanalyst, Edmund Bergler, whose witty and incisive books about marriage and divorce have much to offer the modern reader.

Bergler argued that people often fall in love with someone in order to be able to replay scenes from their childhood. In *Conflicts in Marriage*, a book about 'the unhappy undivorced', he describes the case of a woman pianist who came to him for consultation. She had a successful performance career but her husband disapproved of her giving public concerts and became increasingly strident in his demands that she abandon her career. She had been aware of this disapproval before she married him, so why did she fall in love with him rather than with a more supportive and appreciative man? As a child she was something of a prodigy but her mother had been opposed to her giving public performances. The woman put this down to her mother's 'snobbery' – although, of course, she could have had quite good reasons for not wishing her daughter to be in the public eye at such a young age. Nevertheless, from the child's point of view the mother was a tyrant, bent upon frustrating her daughter's dearest wishes. Bergler is struck by the similar way the woman describes her mother and her husband. Could it be, he asks, that it was precisely this similarity which led her to fall in love with and marry this man? Not in spite of his opposition to her career, but precisely because he repeated her mother's early intransigence. But the intriguing symmetry of the case will remain baffling unless we can describe a mental process which explains the repetition. Why on earth would someone seek to repeat an unhappy experience, and why would someone ensure the repetition of frustration? Bergler thinks that this sort of thing happens too often to be a matter of bad luck – and he puts great stress on the fact that the woman knew, before she married, that this man would oppose her career. Think of the man who falls for a woman he thinks is his intellectual inferior and who continually irritates him with what he regards as foolish remarks. Or the woman who falls for a weak man whom she continually upbraids and nags. These familiar types are deeply exciting to Bergler because they encourage the thought that people often set things up so that they will be annoyed by their partner – annoyed in some specific way that is precious to them, even though it is also – obviously – painful.

But why should this be? Bergler's suggested solution arises from considerations of childhood and from very general considerations of human nature. By nature we seek pleasure and avoid pain. But there are situations – some of them central to the experience of childhood – in which we cannot avoid suffering. A child's desires for satisfaction are often such that they have to be thwarted by a loving parent. The child cannot be taken to the toyshop every day, cannot always have the parent's full attention, has to be potty trained, has to go to bed even though it seems more interesting to stay up. How can a pleasure-seeking creature cope with this? One way is by taking unconscious satisfaction in deprivation. Righteous indignation is perhaps the simplest example of this kind of pleasure. Feeling that one has been wronged may yield a satisfaction of being in the right; it allows one to indulge, with supreme justification, in aggressive feelings. It would be outrageous to feel fury towards a loving mother – but if that mother has just shown herself to be cruel and tyrannical then the feelings do not provoke guilt. The pain of being denied what one longs for becomes mixed with the pleasures of superiority and justified anger.

Thus Bergler can suggest that his pianist was unconsciously seeking out these satisfactions in selecting as a partner a man whom she knew would thwart her. Of course, these satisfactions are, in an important sense, irrational. They come at the cost of multiple dissatisfactions and are entwined with the spoiling of her career. The importance of Bergler's work lies in the way he draws attention to something we would probably rather not recognize: the process of falling in love may be governed not by the intelligent sense of what is good for us but by unconscious forces which cause us to get attached to someone with whom we can – like an addict – repeat a self-harming pleasure. And the exciting thought that 'this is the person for me' may be, ironically, true and yet true only in that we have identified a potential source of our preferred misery.

It would, of course, be unusual to find a relationship in which two people clung to each other only on such a basis – each finding in the other a spur to their masochism. It is more interesting to see this not as the central feature in a relationship but as one ingredient among others. But if we allow the hypothesis any credibility at all it must surely provide yet another reminder of the way in which the suffering which love gives rise to is often connected with the roots of love itself.

This is an account of a strange kind of attraction. But it belongs to a more general thesis about how and why we fall in love. A relationship does not start the day two people meet; it starts in the childhood of each partner. For it is long before they meet that the template of their relationship is established. We learn to love as children. Or, more accurately, we learn a style of relating which governs our adult behaviour when it comes to love.

Central to this thesis is the disturbing contention that we are generally unaware of this underlying style of relating – it governs our adult behaviour without our noticing.

Of course, part of what we learn comes from seeing the way adults relate to each other. It obviously makes a difference if a child regularly sees its parents' enthusiasm and respect for each other rather than mutual contempt and indifference. Equally, a child learns about love through being loved. Take, for example, the case of a child who feels that it can never get its parents full attention except when, by being annoying, it secures at least their irritation. This may establish a pattern which endures into adult life – in which the closeness is equated with annoyance. Such a person might then, in adult relationships, unconsciously provoke their partner so as to recreate this childhood experience.

What this means, in effect, is that the attraction another person has for us depends not just upon their qualities. It also depends upon the way in which we find in them someone with whom we can continue the unfinished business of childhood. We are hugely attracted to this person but the force of attraction might be connected with a quite urgent need to return to some actually rather difficult, even painful, situation in the past. The intensity of the opening stages of love may seem as if it is brought about by the beauty and charm of the other; in fact it may have a darker aspect too. There is something about this person which coheres with an earlier pattern. And it is this coherence which generates excitement, even though – soberly assessed – it may not augur well for our long-term happiness.

Falling in love, then, is a result of two things coming together: the longings which we have and the workings of our imagination. The first draws us out of ourselves in search of another person; the latter intimates that a particular other person may be the one who can satisfy us. When these come together there is an amazing explosion of feeling. All our desires become focused upon that person and we look, dazzled, into those beloved eyes and see – if only for a while – the summation of our own existence and a new world of happiness. Although we have seen that those longings may be darker and more complex than we might like to believe.

imagination (again)

The brilliance of Stendhal's discussion of crystallization may blind us to the fact that he has examined only one way in which imagination may operate in connection with love. He considers the limit case in which imagination is a source of fiction, the power whereby we represent things as other than they actually are. But imagination often has closer ties to reality. Imagination need not stand as an obstacle to clear-sighted perception; on the contrary, it can be a prerequisite for recognition of the less obvious aspects of what is really there. And this is important when we shift our attention from the very opening stage of love (when we fall in love) to consider love in its more long-term aspects. For clearly, if our grasp of the other person were as encrusted with projections as Stendhal suggests, then falling in love could never give way to real intimacy.

Understanding another person is one of the major avenues of closeness. Most people are likely to agree with such a statement; but it is not actually very clear what they would be agreeing to. What is it, after all, to understand another person? One way of approaching this question is to consider the resources we bring to bear when we try to make sense of someone. And one of the key resources we have is, again, imagination. Although this time it is imagination considered in terms rather different from those Stendhal employs.

Ruskin once remarked, in discussing a drawing by Turner, how often appreciation rests upon our recognition of what he called 'the task of the least'. You see that plate, he says, which Turner has sketched in, and placed on the wall in the foreground. See how little of the marked surface it actually occupies. But imagine the picture without it. That small oval which depicts the plate is the key to the whole scheme. It lets our vision come to rest in an otherwise rather empty section of the drawing. Its line echoes, in miniature, the curve of the bay which we see in the distance; thus it serves to integrate the foreground and the middle of the picture. It requires imagination to discern 'the task of the least' – to see the significance of a detail which a hasty eye would easily pass over – but in this case imagination is not departing from what is really there. Imagination enables us to perceive more acutely.

We often think of perception in terms of what are called 'analogue properties' – seeing the shape, colour, texture and comparative size of objects in the world. And it is true that we do not need imagination merely to see what is before us in this sense. But this is a far from complete account of what is there for us to notice. Most obviously we can be more or less responsive to 'relational properties' – for example the relationship between the plate and the bay which Ruskin was so interested in. But to pick up on such relations it is not enough merely to avoid delusion and to set ourselves the task of just seeing what is in front of us. When Ruskin looked at the plate he wondered about its role in the picture, he was alert to the possibility that it might have links to other things in the work. And looking at the drawing with an imaginative eye he was able to discern a real aspect which others might easily miss.

Something similar happens when we look at and think about other people. The capacity to see detail as significant requires that we link an unobtrusive word, gesture or reaction with other elements in a person's life. But of course – as with Turner's plate – it isn't immediately obvious what that little thing should be linked to. Imagination may be thought of in terms of fecundity of options for putting things together. It's not necessarily the case that the imaginative person can see elements other people are unaware of, it's that they think up less expected – and perhaps more revealing – ways of putting together the elements which anyone can observe. This matters when it comes to love, especially falling in love, in a crucial way. Most people are not startlingly beautiful or magically attractive. But someone who seems just moderately nice – to most people – can flower under the imaginative attention of a lover's eye. Not, as Stendhal inclines us to think, because the lover is somehow gilding the other with fictitious charms; but because the kind of attention the lover brings allows less obvious qualities to be seen and appreciated. Just as a muted work of art, like Turner's small sketch, would be quickly passed over by someone alert only to the most obvious signs of artistic bravura, so a muted person (an ordinary person) has attractive qualities which will probably not be evident to a casual observer. In other words, imagination can be allied to acuteness of perception, rather than to distortion. And this function of imagination has its natural application with respect to the quieter, less obvious, features of a person or a work of art.

Our favourite works of art are often those whose less obvious charms yield themselves naturally to the particular tendencies of our imagination. Our individual imaginative characters – the kinds of linkage we are sensitive to, our idiosyncrasies of sensitivity and response – entail that different people will be able to see more or less in any particular work of art. And we tend to like the ones we can see most in. We're not inventing their charms, we just happen to be responsive to them. Almost all loves seem to share this feature. The good patriot is sensitive to the attractions of his native land – he has an eye for the perhaps less obvious appeal of its landscape. There is a coincidence of imaginative style and secret charm. But this holds true also of the parent gazing fondly at the child, of friends enjoying each other's style of thought.

categories

There is a further way in which imagination feeds love –
a way which concerns how we categorize or classify other
people. Consider the case of one of the most celebrated
of friendships: that of Goethe and Schiller. The friendship
between these two men did not have an easy beginning.
Schiller was, in Goethe's eyes, a firebrand radical intent
only on stirring up passions with nothing constructive
to say about how passion should be directed or coped
with. This opinion was only too plausible: Schiller's first
play, *The Robbers*, had been rapturously received in
radical circles. In Schiller's eyes Goethe was undoubtedly
a great writer, but he was also a problem. The apparent
ease of Goethe's life (he had money from his well-
off father and a lucrative position at the Weimar court),
his self-contained sureness and indifference to the opin-
ions of others made him thoroughly unapproachable.
Schiller arrived in Weimar while Goethe was away on
his extended tour of Italy; and although they met a few
times following Goethe's return they had no intimate or
substantial contact.

The initiative to friendship came from Schiller; a brief
discussion about botany, on the doorstep of Schiller's
house, brought into relief the different casts of their

minds. Rather than being put off by this, Schiller turned it brilliantly to account by showing interest in and appreciation of Goethe's mode of thinking, contrasting it with his own, and placing both in a larger historical perspective. After inviting Goethe to assist with the journal *Die Horen* (which Goethe graciously agreed to), Schiller wrote a letter outlining his sense of Goethe's intellectual character – and it was this bold summation which broke into Goethe's reserved and rather isolated life and began a correspondence which continued with extraordinary regularity, ending only with Schiller's death. Schiller draws the intellectual portrait of those whose minds tend to start from the particular and concrete and then undertake a synthetic project of drawing together the multitude of their perceptions, never losing sight of the answerability of generalization to particular fact. Thus Goethe always wanted to find the primal plant – not just an idea, but an actual object which would constitute the basic general nature of all plants. The question is not whether Goethe was right in this undertaking, but what it shows about the character of his mind – his longing for the particular and the concrete, his devotion to his own experience and desire always to see things with his own eyes. Schiller contrasts this with his own mental temper, which aims, on the contrary, to find incontrovertible and highly generalized starting-points which are essentially non-experiential in character.

In his essay *On Naïve and Sentimental Poetry*, which grew out of the letter to Goethe, he goes on to elaborate a whole attitude to nature and life which is implicit in these two divergent starting-points. Schiller notes how sometimes we are moved by the mere recognition of something as natural – it has a poignancy and pathos for us, because on the one hand we feel removed from it and on the other hand it stands as a call to what we might become (not in imitation, but in a new way, finding a new kind of harmony, simplicity and straightforwardness).

What is revealed here is the imaginative shift which Schiller accomplished in the way he classified Goethe. He managed to move from the kind of categories we use all the time: rich, lucky, aloof, and to come up with a much more interesting – and powerful – way of classifying this man and indeed himself. But of course it took imagination to make this move and to come up with a better way of thinking about his relationship to Goethe. Although Schiller was being imaginative in finding a new frame in which to place Goethe, he wasn't distorting his rather daunting friend in doing so. Schiller wasn't simply making up a more appealing story. What he was doing was searching amongst the many truths about Goethe for the ones which would enable a friendship between them to flower – as indeed it did. Goethe was indeed well-off, lucky and aloof, but of course he was many other things as well. A key point about Schiller's way of thinking about people was that it included himself; he could come to see himself as sharing something important with Goethe – a concern with the relation between particular and general – even though they approached this problem from different starting-points. And this frame was one which Goethe in turn was able to appropriate so that he could now see Schiller as a valued companion rather than as a dangerous rival.

Of course, this example is highly intellectual – we don't need to develop theories of human nature and write essays about the essence of poetry in order to be more imaginative about how we see others. Goethe himself had made use of just such an imaginative resource during a love affair he had in Rome a couple of years before he got to know Schiller. In the *Roman Elegies*, once considered among his more *risqué* works, Goethe tells, in a series of short poems, the story of this love affair in Rome with a young woman he calls Faustina. Her charm, for him, was hugely augmented by the way he saw in her the life of the city he so loved. He was entranced by the idea that to her the Pantheon was not some almost legendary temple, the goal of a pilgrimage (as it had been to him), but just the church round the corner which she might pass on the way to the market to buy some goat's cheese. She was the symbol of living familiarity with classical culture, not as objects of recondite learning, but as the wonderful setting for everyday existence. He saw in her graceful simplicity and straightforwardness, when it came to sex, the wholesomeness of the Roman republic. He saw in her the modern representative of the mistresses of the classic love poets.

It is to Schiller, too, that we owe a moving evocation of a further role imagination plays in love. His ode *Antici-pation* (to which Schubert gave one of his finest settings) describes the thoughts and emotions of a lover sitting by a window, awaiting the arrival of his beloved; it is probably based on an experience of his own waiting for Charlotte von Lengefeld, the woman he was soon to marry. At every moment a slight sound or movement in the garden makes him think she has come at last – but no, he realizes it was only the wind in the branches of the trees, an apple dropping in the orchard, or the glimmer of a swan on the lake. But in his disappointment he enjoys a stronger and surer grasp of his love for her. Why? Because anticipation, if conducted imaginatively (as it is here), doesn't just mean hanging around muttering: 'Where is she, when is she coming?' It involves thinking: 'Was that her footstep? I love the way she walks, she seems to carry herself so lightly.' That is, it involves dwelling upon just what it is one is waiting for: the other comes alive under the benign influence of such thoughts. The lover, in this beautiful song, sees the whole of nature joining in his passion. He wants the trees to embrace her protectively, he wants the gentle breeze to enjoy the warmth of her cheeks; he begs night and silence to come quickly and provide the perfect sympathetic setting for their love. And he sees his own love as continuous with an eroticized nature: doesn't the wind kiss the flower; don't grapes and pears swell under the loving influence of the sun?

The way the lover uses nature in this poetic example has, of course, a distinguished cultural history. It was a major obsession of the era to see in nature a reflection of human passions; this in turn was a special development of the medieval view which regarded all of nature in symbolic terms. But the interest of the ode, for me, does not lie in the specific images employed. Rather it is the way in which the lover spins out – and enlarges – his passion by aligning it with whatever comes conveniently to hand. This is the opposite of the climax and discharge of passion which brings feeling to a close. On the contrary, imagination in this case seeks to keep the passion growing in the mind of the lover.

15

conflict and interpretation

The positive view of understanding another person – the view that this is, to a significant degree, possible – gives rise to a serious conflict. For a commitment to this possibility opens the way for a divergence between such understanding and the way a person thinks of himself or herself. That is, we have to take into account the possibility that a person does not have a high degree of self-understanding (as we have just seen).

When it comes to lovers, the situation is even more difficult. Adults, of course, necessarily feel that they know their own interests – this is part of their reflective self-awareness – and the resentment caused by a lover presenting and trying to promote an alternative course can be intense. (Or the adult may feel that, while a certain course would be in their interest, it is simply not within their power to abide by it, and have come to accept a relatively lower achievement of their own good.)

The suggestion that love is deep carries the implication that it emerges from deep within us and that it reaches something deep within us. It carries with it an image of the personality as layered. It is as if the personality has a core, around which more superficial and accidental features of personality accrue.

It is precisely this model of personality which Henry James puts into the hands of his male protagonist, Basil Ransom, in *The Bostonians*. Ransom is deeply attracted to a young woman, Verena Tarrant, who has an amazing gift for public speaking. She has grown up in an atmosphere of radicalism and public agitation and has recently been more or less adopted by an earnest and affluent young Bostonian, Olive Chancellor. Olive (Basil's distant cousin) has focused Verena's emotions and abilities on the cause of the emancipation of women. As it happens, this is a cause to which Basil Ransom is unsympathetic. He seeks to understand his attachment by distinguishing between Verena's 'essential' personality (sweet, vivacious, empathetic, self-possessed) and the 'accidental' set of concerns to which she has been directed (opening the professions and universities to women, legal reform, and so on). This has occurred through what he considers the misfortune of her upbringing and associations. He therefore thinks that he can detach the young woman from her current concerns and that in doing so he will not only not injure her but positively liberate her real character, which has been distorted and obscured. It turns out, in the course of the novel, that he succeeds in convincing Verena of this too; she herself comes to see her public speaking career (which has been very successful) as a diversion – indeed a vulgarization – of her real interests.

The beauty of the example should not be missed because of how we view the cause Verena advocates. The truth of its importance in the world does not entail that it must be the thing Verena should consider her vocation. So Ransom could be right that her concern with it does not reflect her real personality (even if we, unlike him, consider it an admirable interest).

Belief in a core 'real self' which can be seriously at odds with a surface of socially acquired characteristics gives rise to a number of problems. Firstly it lends itself with embarrassing ease to misuse. It is only too tempting – on the strength of such a thesis – to suppose that whatever one finds awkward about a person simply belongs to the surface and could be renounced by them, while whatever we would prefer them to be is assigned to the permanent substrate. The imagined benefit of being true to this substrate licenses all kinds of violence to the persona we encounter.

A further difficulty is more theoretical: the distinction itself does not tell us, in any detail, how we are to decide what is essential to a persona and what is accidental. We could operate with a minimalist view which sees almost nothing of their apparent personality as really 'them'. But what entitles us to this ontological surgery, to this drastic reduction of what is really there in a personality?

However, neither of these problems suffices to show that the view is, in its outlines, fundamentally misconceived. Indeed, judging from the inside – taking our own private case as exemplary – it seems all to obvious that we do in fact embrace (and want to embrace) a differentiation along these lines. It is actually an avenue of hope to be able to think that my irascibility is not 'my real self' but an overlay, and that it could indeed be diminished without damaging me – indeed it would release the real me from my current position as hostage to certain acquired and circumstantial characteristics. The fact that the distinction lends itself to misuse and that it is hard to know how to apply it is a call to caution and care in application, not to the abandonment of the guiding thought.

But certain caveats apply: there is limited ground for assuming (as Ransom does) that what is real is necessarily nicer or more appealing than what is acquired and circumstantial. It might be that, deep down, I am insecure and selfish. And, indeed, this is a possibility which James explores in the narrative. The other character who is deeply attached to Verena, Olive Chancellor, appears in her public persona as self-possessed and as having a stoic indifference to the views of the world and a remarkable capacity to content herself with the private conviction that her passions are just. As the story unfolds, however, a different, deeper, part of her character is revealed. We see that Olive is profoundly insecure, that she longs to be seen – by everyone – as a success, that she needs to impose herself on others and have them docile before her. In other words, there is much that is deep about Olive which is not appealing.

This story shows us a heroic ideal of what it is to understand another person: it involves having a clear conception of what that person's real needs and qualities are – a conception which can be radically at variance with the self-image of that person. And it also sponsors a heroic conception of what love involves. It involves helping that person to adjust their self-image, bringing it into line with the truth – of which the lover is the guardian.

This way of construing the lover's knowledge need not be wrong. Why should we deny that there can be cases such as this? But it does bring to light certain major difficulties which knowledge can generate in love. Our sense of who another person really is can be massively inflected by our own concerns. It is all too easy to see Ransom, in the story we have been considering, as simply imposing his preferred image of Verena upon her. Of course he thinks he is right, but conviction is hardly the criterion of truth. This story reminds us – if we need reminding – of the central place of knowledge in love. Knowledge of the other plays a vital part in one of the oldest understandings of love, to which we now turn.

the good of
the other

One of the oldest definitions of love, and one which has persisted at the core of thinking on the subject, comes from Aristotle, in Book 8 of the *Nichomachean Ethics*. Writing about friendship, he defines *philia* as a desire to do 'what is good for the other not for one's own sake, but for theirs'. Love is connected with kindness. Clearly this is not all that is at stake in love but, in a single quiet sentence, Aristotle gestures at the practical territory in which love operates. He produces this definition of love in the context of a discussion of friendship; rather than compromise it as an account of love, this provides a principled ground for seeing friendship, at its best, as a species of love.

In the earlier chapters of this book we have been concerned with what the lover wants from the beloved – namely, a special kind of recognition – and with what is seen, more or less accurately, in the beloved – the inventory of attractions. Aristotle's definition reminds us that love is also a practical matter: that loving someone doesn't just mean sitting about thinking how nice they are; it also involves caring for that person.

Aristotle puts altruism – acting for the good of someone else – at the centre of love. This involves a remarkable shift in the ordinary pattern of motivation. Normally we expect people to act according to a vision of their own self-interest. But Aristotle suggests that in friendship and in love another person comes to be a 'second self' – meaning that concern with what is good for them directs our actions just as readily as concern with what is good for us.

We must at once close off a wide avenue of misunderstanding which is opened by Aristotle's specific (and to us strange) use of 'good'. The good of the other is very closely linked, in his mind, to happiness. He thinks that happiness – long-term satisfaction – is the natural ambition of life; it is the 'good' of human existence: the goal at which we all naturally aim. The *Ethics* is basically a study of what it takes to be happy. Aristotle identifies a range of 'virtues' which are, collectively, the best recipe we have for achieving this goal. He takes a thoroughly empirical approach. Look around at the people who are happy and unhappy and see what generalizations can be drawn: this is his strategy. He thinks that, on the whole, people who are intelligent, generous, self-controlled, sociable and courageous (who don't give up too easily) are more likely to end up happy than those who lack these qualities. Happiness, therefore, depends to a large extent upon your personal qualities. Without these, no quantity of worldly goods or prestige will do anything other than deepen your misery.

To seek the good of the other is, in the end, to seek their happiness. This is what altruism, and love, come to. In modern discussions of love, altruism sometimes gets a bad name, and not surprisingly. We have become highly sensitive to the ways in which people, especially women, can 'love too much'. This happens when one partner takes a subordinate role in a relationship – endlessly sacrificing their own concerns and interests to what suits the other. Ultimately this leads to the destruction of the sacrificed personality, so that the subordinate lover has no authentic concerns and is simply a support mechanism for the other party. More dramatically, there are cases in which one party (a woman, usually) hopes to reform the other through love and invests more and more devotion, effort and self-sacrifice in a failing cause.

But if we view Aristotle's notion of altruism in the way we elaborated it a moment ago, it is evident that these kinds of situations do not actually correspond to the point he is making. In fact his aim is to distinguish altruism, and love, from this sort of domestic tragedy. His point, of course, turns on a distinction between 'doing what is good for the other' and 'doing what the other wants'. For Aristotle it is axiomatic that people can be wrong about what is good for them; that is, they can be wrong about what will make them happy. This is one of the key reasons why there is so much unhappiness in the world.

To be altruistic, therefore, is not necessarily to be accommodating – it may involve going against your partner's wishes and inclinations. Although pandering to the whims of your partner can placate their immediate distress, it can't lead them to long-term satisfaction, to happiness. Aristotle is announcing a rather pessimistic thesis. Although love aims at making the other happy, love is not a particularly powerful tool in this endeavour. If he is right in stressing the capacities of character which underwrite the possibility of happiness, then this pessimism is justified. Love alone can't make another adult intelligent, generous, courageous, persistent and sociable – unless they are very close to possessing these qualities in the first place. Much of the time we will be unable to make another person happy, because that person lacks the essential characteristics which make their own happiness possible.

On this view it is futile, and worthless, to love someone who is not virtuous (in Aristotle's special sense of virtue). For in that case the aim of love will always be frustrated: the desire to make the other happy will never come to fruition, not because one is insufficiently ardent or self-sacrificing but because the character flaws of the other cut them off from happiness.

This kind of stern thinking can be extremely salutary for people who are prone to blame themselves too much for the failure of a relationship. Anyone who has taken to heart a magical view of love (love can conquer all, all you need is love) must be left thinking that they didn't love sufficiently well if a relationship fails. Since, as they think, love can achieve miracles if only it is strong enough, the only explanation of failure lies in the quality of one's love. Aristotle makes a powerful point against this way of thinking.

This approach also has something to say to one of the most powerful fantasies which grips us as we fall in love: 'my happiness depends upon you, only you and your love can make me happy'. Against this Aristotle makes the sobering point that, in fact, one's happiness does not lie so dramatically in the hands of another person. And unless one already possesses certain virtues (that is, the kinds of disposition which make long-term satisfaction viable) then there really isn't very much another person can do.

If love aims at happiness, and happiness depends upon virtue, then the central thing we want to know about a prospective partner is this: what virtues do they possess and what are their defects of character? Virtue and discernment are, therefore, the pillars of love: the novels of Jane Austen provide a perfect rendition of the Aristotelian conception of love.

charity

One of the key episodes in Tolstoy's *Anna Karenin* occurs when Levin – the hero – hears that his elder brother, Nikolai, is dying. Nikolai has led a dissipated life, moved in radical circles far from the aristocratic milieu into which he was born, and exhausted his inheritance – partly by supporting unsuccessful philanthropic projects. He is an alcoholic and lives with a former prostitute. Although the brothers have quarrelled – and the fault seems to lie squarely on the side of Nikolai – Levin decides to go and visit his brother. At first he is horrified that his young wife, Kitty, wishes to accompany him: 'The mere idea of his wife, Kitty, in the same room with a common wench set him shuddering with repulsion and horror.'

In the end, however, Kitty does accompany her husband. The situation in which they find his brother is appalling. 'In the dirty little room, the painted dado round the walls filthy with spittle, the atmosphere evil-smelling and stifling, lay a body covered with a quilt.' His brother's body is horrifically emaciated; the only signs of life are his twitching mouth and a severe, reproachful look in his glittering eyes. Nikolai is not a sympathetic character. Earlier we have seen him treating his companion, Masha, with casual cruelty.

Kitty becomes marvellously active, refusing to be put off. She introduces cleanliness, order, calm; she cleans Nikolai's bedsores and tries to soothe his grotesque body. But Kitty's charity is not merely active – it's not just that she actively improves the dying man's condition, so that he can retain some dignity, it's rather that she refuses to limit her attention to the external features of the situation. It is as if she sees past his surface character – his severity, envy, bad temper and general degradation – and sees him as deserving kindness, consideration, cleanliness and comfort. It is not that she doesn't notice the off-putting features, but these are not what her attention is focused upon. She sees past them to a decent, unlucky, unhappy man – and she acts in response to that. The charity, therefore, is as much present in her way of seeing him as it is in her material efforts. Here, love is moved not by excellence but by weakness and need.

In this scene Tolstoy is depicting a vision of love which derives from the Sermon on the Mount. In this sermon, Christ articulates God's love for the weak, the poor and the dispossessed. This is a loving attitude which is replicated in Kitty's attention to Nikolai. But its specific mechanisms were described by St Paul in the First Letter to the Corinthians – one of the central documents in the Western history of love. Paul's account of the loving attitude (his attempt to say what it is to love) is couched in a thesis about interpretation. To love is to interpret another person with charity. It is to believe the best about them which is consistent with the facts – and of course we habitually go beyond the facts when we find fault with or condemn another. And, as a consequence, the one who loves is slow to anger and quick to forgive.

This is completely logical. Anger and resentment are frequently founded upon what we suppose another person has intended, rather than on what we actually know about their motives. Charity, therefore, need not ascribe benign motives, but keeps open the possibility that one doesn't know what really goes on in another's heart of hearts.

Burns's famous plea for charity of interpretation (he had been condemned for adultery) is exactly on target:

> Then gently scan your brother Man,
> Still gentler sister Woman;
> Tho' they may gang a kennin wrang [go a little astray],
> To step aside is human:
> One point must still be greatly dark,
> The moving *Why* they do it;
> And just as lamely can ye mark,
> How far perhaps they rue it.

We don't know, he says, what inner compulsion someone labours under, nor how far they resist – they may have held themselves in check many times but this goes unnoticed; we don't know what loneliness or sorrow may drive someone to excess. This ignorance, he argues, should qualify our inclination to condemn, to get angry or resentful; it should increase our goodwill.

Returning to Nikolai's deathbed scene in *Anna Karenin*, we might construe Kitty's actions as founded upon a charitable interpretation of Nikolai. This makes a crucial difference. To be kind to someone whom one regards as undeserving is an act of condescension; it is not a relationship between equals. But under the charity of interpretation, the other is not seen as undeserving. Nikolai first is returned his dignity in her eyes before it is aided physically by her efforts as a nurse.

Of course, Tolstoy is here dealing with a case far removed from relationships. Kitty is loving towards Nikolai, but she's not in love with him; she doesn't love him the way she loves her husband. However, it seems clear that in this sickbed scene we are presented with a theme which enters into romantic relationships.

Our thinking about love – and our experience of love – exists at the intersection of the traditions which derive from Aristotle and St Paul. The first concentrates on a person's virtues – on their healthy capacity for happiness. The second invites us to a charitable interpretation which seeks out good qualities underneath the evident failings and inadequacies – and takes a sympathetic view of those failings. Without wanting to minimize the tension between these two visions of love, we can see many points at which – in the course of actual experience – they work in the most important ways in harmony. It is rare that a person falls clearly on one side of the divide or the other; either an Aristotelian paragon or a Nikolai-like reprobate. Most people are, it goes without saying, sometimes pathetic and sometimes quite competent. In other words, any loving relationship will probably need to work with both conceptions of love. And because this duality applies to oneself, as well as to one's partner, a profound kind of reciprocity is at stake. If, at certain moments, I adopt a Pauline attitude to my partner it is partly because I identify with the need for charitable interpretation; it is precisely this kind of interpretation which I stood in need of yesterday, or will be in need of tomorrow. Obviously, this kind of reciprocity requires us to hold in mind a complex image of our own nature. It requires that, in times of strength, our periods of passivity, of vulnerability, remain alive to us as sources of compassion. A contemporary vision of love, therefore, aligns love both with liking and with kindness. 'Affectionate kindness', a simple phrase, is a definition of love which reminds us of some of its most important themes.

love and the
meaning of life

How important is love in life? In the West, the highest status was given to love by Christianity. At the core of this system is the idea that God's relation to the world is governed by love. God is love; the creation of the universe was an act of love – the role of humanity is freely to love God. Genuine love cannot be coerced; the role of mankind is not to be compelled to love God, but freely come to love him. But for this freedom to be real, it must be possible for us to turn from loving God and direct our attentions and desires elsewhere. It is the problematic connection between love and freedom which governs the human condition.

Love of God, according to this view, has to be realized in one's love for God's creation – for other people. 'Whatever you do to the least of my brothers, you do to me' is the core Christian statement of this position. Because, in the Christian view, God loves all humanity, we are called upon to love those who seem to be unlovable. That is why we must love our enemies as well as our friends, why we must forgive not seven times but seventy times seven. In so doing we are participating in God's inexhaustible love of humanity. Sin, wrongdoing, is essentially a refusal of love – either to give or accept love.

Sin, therefore, is not so much an offence against God, but harm to oneself. Part of the Christian position is that human beings are, on their own, incapable of such high demands. It is only through divine assistance – grace – that we are made able to love so widely and so unselfishly. Grace is, essentially, a personal manifestation of God's love for the individual. While this has often been presented in an external form (taking communion, going to confession), the underlying principle is clear: what is crucial in communion or confession is that the individual participant finds in the sacrament a revelation of God's love for them as an individual. God sent his only son to die for you – because he loves you; God forgives your weaknesses – because he loves you. So in each case the intended response is gratitude and a renewal of love in the individual.

This account of existence places love at the centre of life. We live in order to grow in love – that is the meaning and purpose of each individual life. Nothing matters as much as this. Such an explicit and comprehensive thesis about the role of love in life might seem to tie love inescapably to a particular outlook, in this case to an elaborate theology. What would happen if the theology were to be pushed aside or discredited? The curious fact is that love has also played an important part in many other non-religious and even anti-religious systems of thought.

Take for example the early Romantic plays of Schiller, which deal with the politics of freedom. In those works, the hero is always one who loves passionately and tenderly and whose love is thwarted by society in some cruel way. In society greed, cynicism and the pursuit of power triumph over love. In *Politics and Passion*, first performed in 1784, Schiller traces the fate of a love which grows between the son of the prime minister of a small German principality and the daughter of a mere musician. The true lovers are separated in part by the impositions of class difference. But the prime minister also wants to marry his son to the prince's mistress for political reasons. The procurement of such a marriage of convenience will secure the father's influence at court and brilliantly enhance the prospects of the son. In the drama these worldly considerations are played out against the sweetness and purity of the son's deep love for the musician's daughter. Love stands in danger of being destroyed by vanity, greed and the desire for political power – and, indeed, is ultimately crushed by these hostile forces.

Schiller thus aligns love with freedom, but also with goodness. The designs of the prime minister are ruthlessly indifferent to anything but his own prestige; but what allows him to have such designs is the prevailing order. A despotic prince, answerable only to his own pleasures, can be manipulated by one who has the ear of his mistress. A father can impose his will upon his son because he has the legal authority to do so. In other words, true love brings into focus the corruption of the prevailing order. And such corruption operates against true love. Thus love plays an extremely important part in Schiller's political thinking. The experience of love helps us to see the reality of corruption. And one of the things which is wrong with corruption is that it has to crush love in order to achieve its own ends. We need to be free if we are to love.

This philosophical position – concerning the relations

between love, freedom and justice – makes no mention of theology; yet like the Christian position we considered above, it regards love as a central phenomenon in life, one around which other key ideas fall into place. Schiller also builds into the play a distinction between pure, or true, love and a counterfeit version. The prince seeks to display his passion to his mistress, and to minister to her vanity, by purchasing some exceedingly expensive jewels for her. To pay for them he sells a number of his subjects into a foreign army – a slave trade notoriously practised by certain princes of the period. The present of the jewels shows up the unreality of the prince's love for his mistress – if they really loved one another it would be unnecessary to multiply the sufferings of the world in order to gratify vanity and provide a trivial token of esteem. In true love, it is the intimate interaction of two hearts, not the giving of such gifts, that counts. So here again a vision of love enters into a political and ethical thesis.

Schiller's philosophy of love, as presented in *Politics and Passion*, is idealistic. It belongs to a group of theories in which we see the problems of existence as deriving mainly from corrupt forms of government. These are problems which could, in principle, be removed by political and legal reform. They are not deep problems – however crushing they may be for the central characters in the play. A more profound analysis of the human situation – with regard to love – is advanced by Schiller a decade later in his *Letters on the Aesthetic Education of Mankind*, which first appeared in 1795. There Schiller movingly writes, in the sixth letter, of the 'fragmentation' and 'specialization' of human nature. Instead of developing as whole and well-rounded individuals we have to give one-sided emphasis to particular aspects of our being in order to get on in the world. This is damaging when it comes to love. For Schiller believes that love requires the integration of all our powers: we have to be sensual, but also understanding; we need to be able to relax with our beloved, but must equally exercise self-control; we have to mix spontaneity with foresight; passionate, devouring sexual desire has to be tempered with respect. It is, however, precisely such a balance of potentially conflicting capacities which is lost in specialization and fragmentation. In this way, love stands as the test case of the psychological health of an individual and of a society.

Schiller's theory of love, and of the problems we face as we try to love, is of particular interest because it draws together themes which were later to be given extensive individual treatment by Marx and Freud. According to Marx, humanity – and love – could only come into their own in the wake of wholesale reformation of society. At the centre of Marx's critique of capitalism is the idea that under a capitalist economic structure human nature is deformed, or 'alienated' from itself. Economic relations don't just impinge upon what we can do – as social relations impinge, in Schiller's view, upon how we can live our lives. They do something more powerful and strange: they actually limit what we can be. What is wrong with capitalism is not so much that it fosters an unjust distribution of wealth but rather that it damages the personalities of all those who live within it, cutting each individual off from the realization of their true nature, giving rise to internal – as well as external –

obstacles to love. There is a important resonance here for modern life. If we have to devote our best energies, and almost all of our time, to making a living, and if in doing so we have to become highly competitive, or ruthless, we don't have much of ourselves left over for love. We can only love on the margins of our lives and with the residue of our capacities. This takes on a tragic dimension when we can no longer believe that a better economic system is viable. Love, which stands as the natural goal of living, is massively subordinated to the pursuit of the means of living.

In Freud's view – to take up the other theme which is present in Schiller's thought – the obstacles to love are more intimate and derive from individual, personal history. To sketch Freud's views as briefly as possible, he regards the goal of life, the sign of psychological health, as the capacity to work and love. Many factors in one's personality, however, conspire to make this goal hard to achieve. One of the problems, when it comes to love, is transference. The idea, here, is that we invest the people we encounter – particularly those we get close to – with characteristics which are not really their own but which derive from our own earlier relationships.

We 'construct' the other person – in our minds – not on the basis of observation but according to a pre-given model of our own. For example, when one's lover asks, 'Why did you do that?', the question can be heard as an open inquiry or as an implied criticism. Which way one hears it is governed not by the words themselves but by an assumption about the motives and attitudes of the questioner. There is a type of bore who systematically imagines that others are interested in what they have to say. A shy person may construct everyone they meet according to a template of indifference or hostility. Construction is an unconscious process – one which we are not only unaware of but which we positively resist becoming aware of. It is hard to love well, and easy to love badly, if one's sense of another person is dominated by unconscious fantasies about who they are. The ability to love well is really an indication that one's engagements with others are not dominated by such fantasies – one can, therefore, judge a person or a situation on their merits.

Freud believed that these unconscious fantasies about who the other person is derive from our earliest loves – with our parents, and narcissistically, with ourselves. Hence the lover may really be trying to find a mother or father or another self in the beloved, without being aware that this is going on. And, of course, such fantasy figures will not merely be the objects of one's longing, but also of fears and aggression and vengeance. Relationships guided by such fantasies can – obviously – be intense, but their detachment from who the other person really is must be disastrous in the long term. Hence the ability to love in the long term requires the resolution of this unconscious material. Hence the aspiration that psychotherapy which investigates and tries to modify unconscious fantasies will make us more able to love successfully.

What is striking about all these diverse views, from Christ to Freud, is that they all make love central to the ideal of life, but in their individual ways remind us how difficult it is to realize this ideal. In each case, love is seen in relation to a particular set of problems – the problems which each thinker sees as the most pressing or most interesting in life. But in each case the notion of love on offer is enriched because it is seen as illuminating the condition of life: it is in part thinking about love which makes us see difficulties as difficulties, because they are obstacles to the realization of love.

I have not attempted to rebut any of these lines of argument, although such attempts are frequently made. I'm not interested in whether we should absolutely adhere to, or completely reject, any of these views. Instead I am trying to work with an approach which might be called 'pandoxist'.

The pantheist doesn't locate divinity in any particular being, but finds divinity expressed, in different ways, throughout the world. A 'pandoxist' doesn't locate all the important insights and truths about life in a single system, but tries to seize upon the multitude of truths and insights which are located in many distinct – and sometimes antagonistic – positions. This is partly supported by the opinion that most great systems of thought are founded upon lasting insights – although the articulation of these concerns frequently involves exaggeration; *an* insight is presented as *the* insight. A second support comes in the reflection that we generally don't need to be completely consistent in our thinking. The pursuit of consistency has, of course, made the running in philosophy since Plato – indeed the whole thrust of Socrates' mode of engagement is to test the consistency of his interlocutor's beliefs. But when we think about love we are not, generally, in pursuit of a single, complete theory of love – a point which I argued at the start of the book. Rather we are, as individual thinkers and lovers, attempting to enrich our repertoire of ideas: to see the power of a point of view or the unexpected richness of an apparently trivial suggestion. Because the experience of love is, within each individual, composed of varied moods, moments and problems, we need thoughts which will be helpful at these different times and in different situations. Thus there may be moods in which we can make use of a Marxian insight and others at which we would be better turning to Freud. And if Marx and Freud are, strictly speaking, incompatible formal theories, so much the worse for the narrow application of particular theories to life.

In each of the theories we have looked at, love stands as a 'regulative' ideal. A regulative ideal is one which is reasonably founded in an understanding of human nature. Justice and freedom are similarly ideals. Even though perfect justice may be impossible in the world, our assessment of whether something is just or not is guided by reference to a rational account of what justice is. Regulative ideals don't seek to describe how things actually are; instead they refer us to a point of view from which we can assess ourselves and the world. In other words, if we acknowledge an ideal as regulative we accept that it won't be fully realized – indeed, that is not the point. The account of ideal love isn't meant to describe something which could actually be fulfilled.

The vague – and slightly thrilling – idea of 'the meaning of life' traditionally referred to the purpose of life. Thus, as we have seen, for Augustine the purpose of being alive was to orient one's longings towards God – life is the arena in which we have to learn to do this one supremely important thing. But mostly what we think of as the 'meaning' of life concerns the style of the private auto-biography we each write and which records how we 'see' ourselves. Whether this autobiography reads as a narrative of progress in which difficulties are tran-scended, or is chaotic, is the test of whether one's life seems to be meaningful or not. Meaning is something we find, or fail to find, as we follow through this project. We can see how love figures here: love is a major theme, but how we see our experience of love depends upon our general thinking. If, for example, we work with extremely high expectations of love we impose a tragic style upon our self-perceptions: for our experience of love will always be seen under an aspect of failure – failure focused upon ourselves or others. Hence the more subtle our thinking about love, the more intelligently we discrimi-nate ideals from reality, the more interesting our autobi-ography becomes.

incommensurable desires

It is simply not the case that all our desires or demands cohere with each other. This is profoundly connected with one of the most unhelpful features of the human condition: we tend to underestimate the importance of familiar things just because they are familiar, and to overestimate how much we would enjoy other things just because they are currently unavailable. This is the law fixed in the cliché that 'the grass is always greener on the other side' – a formula which exemplifies itself. The very familiarity of the thought lessens our respect for it. From within a stable relationship the charms of adventures and change can seem almost irresistible. To those who have the freedom for such a course of action, the freedom itself seems worthless; they long instead for security and deep involvement. Rather than just judging human nature as congenitally stupid we should, I think, see these conflicts as exemplifying a plurality of significant, and largely incompatible, concerns. Freedom is an important good, but so too is security; the taste for enlargement of self-knowledge and the curiosity which feeds a desire for adventure are genuinely valuable. The goal of independence is important, but so too is the capacity to submerge one's independence in a commitment to another.

These are tensions within ourselves which can hardly allow of simple resolution. Even if we rationally (and sensibly) come to a conclusion one way or another, we still have to live with the consequence that something important has been sacrificed. And the scar of this sacrifice lives on in our experience of love, introducing a permanent pain and dissatisfaction into otherwise very healthy relationships. Love, then, can never be the coming together of two perfectly compatible creatures. We are not like jigsaw pieces which can, if only we find the correct piece, lock together in perfect accord. It is as if each person actually belongs to several jigsaws at once and hence fits perfectly into none.

So far we have considered the tensions in a single person as they emerge from the simple fact that we have multiple desires and interests which are not easily reconciled in reality – because fulfilling one precludes fulfilling another. As if this were not bad enough, there is a deeper and more potent form of inner conflict that remains to be examined. It is to this we now proceed.

Among the most disturbing features of the experience of love is the way in which it can be precisely towards those to whom we are most attached that we have the most intense feelings of revulsion, criticism or desire to denigrate and hurt. These may function at distinct levels of self-awareness; for example we may feel completely justified and hence unaware of an intimate connection between our love and our anger. This connection of apparently contrary attitudes can seem impossible or offensive if we think of love as wholly good. If, however, we complicate our conception of love and admit that it involves such things as idealization, intensity of demand to be met and recognized, that it is 'archaic' and carries with it fears and anxieties as well as esteem and affection, then this concatenation will appear more understandable. (Though no less painful when we live through it.) One of the obstacles to such a complex view of love has been its articulation in the New Testament, which presents us with a wholly positive – and superhuman – vision of love. For the divine love of man is not engendered as one person's love for another; it does not have an origin in insecurity, it does not carry into itself all the complexities of character that are the fate of any individual human being. It presents, for better and worse, an ideal image of how we would like to love – not merely in its intensity of self-forgetting and devotion to the other, but in its separation from the highly imperfect way in which we come to love. (Which is not to suggest that theologians or Christian writers have been blind to this difficulty.)

However, it is not just in exceptional cases that love is conjoined with episodes of hatred. It is so frequently the case that we might be tempted to suppose that it is pure love which constitutes the exception, and that such purity, rather than being the natural condition, is something which requires special explanation.

The notion of ambivalence – the notion that loving and hating frequently stand in an intimate connection – is widely used in psychoanalysis. Freud's account of the Oedipus complex is a key instance of this. He supposes that the young boy who is passionately attached to his mother comes to think that his father is a rival for the affection of his beloved mother. There are, Freud believes, many consequences that follow from this belief. Among these are the ambivalent attitudes the little boy then feels towards his parents. His mother is still loved, but she rejects him in favour of the father, and she is hated for that. His father is still an object of love, but he is also the one who has (the boy thinks) taken mummy away and is feared as a vengeful and jealous rival. In each case a pattern of ambivalence is established: the same object is both loved and hated. And ambivalence surfaces in other accounts of early emotional life. According to Melanie Klein, one of the most imaginative and forceful of Freud's successors, we can observe ambivalence in very young babies as they feed. When the feeding is going well the breast (or the bottle – it doesn't matter which because the baby still, we think, experiences the bottle as part of the mother) is an object of love. But when there is any obstacle to the baby's desires (if there is some difficulty in starting the feed or when the feed is finished) the breast becomes an object of hatred. To start with, Klein thinks, the baby experiences the shift from satisfaction to dissatisfaction as the replacement of a good mother by a bad mother. But it is not long before these two mothers are seen to be the same person; hence the baby has both feelings for one person – ambivalence. And the limited perspective of the child makes such a mixed view of the parents inevitable. A tired child will experience the parent's necessary manoeuvre to get it into bed as a horrible persecution revealing their complete lack of sympathy. Jealousy and hatred can – obviously – also be aroused in the child by the parents' relations to other children. It looks to a three-year-old as if the parents' necessary attention to, and enthusiasm for, a new baby is a deliberate rejection.

Much of the resulting pain of adult life can be traced back to the ways in which the child deals with ambivalence. Either element of the conjunction may be disowned. The child might ease its emotional situation by turning away from the aggressive, hating elements in its feelings for its mother and father. This allows the child to feel a pure love; and this, it might be said, is the psychological background that makes the pure love of Christianity so appealing. But the price of excluding the negative aspect can be high. An older child might turn away from the loving aspect and embrace a cynical, dismissive attitude to anything tender or sweet – seeing that as babyish or sentimental.

One way of using these speculations is to draw a genealogical history of adult love; that is, to suggest that these more or less inevitable experiences of ambivalence lay down the pattern to which later loves conform. An adult relationship reawakens the fears and disappointments which occurred in childhood – even though we may not be explicitly aware of this. Or we try to reverse the suffering of those early situations, or in some way dispel ambivalence. We might become promiscuous in order to show that we don't care whether the other loves us back (revenge upon the betraying mother); or we might sadistically identify with the aggression of an angry parent, enacting the aggression ourselves so as not to have to fear it.

Another way of taking these Freudian speculations is to see them as suggestive of just how readily a feeling of love generates its opposite. For if we are right in seeing love as founded on longing and possessiveness directed at another, then it is almost always going to be the case that the other person will generate severe difficulties for these passions.

What the account of ambivalence implies about love is this: it is impossible to have a loving relationship which does not involve negative aspects. This is not because we are insufficiently skilled when it comes to finding the 'right partner'. It is because a perfectly right partner will still evoke fears and anxieties in us, will still – because of connections back to the roots of love and fear in child-hood – become an object of envy or jealousy, will still be the privileged object of our aggression and disappoint-ment. Indeed to think that one may have escaped this scenario is perhaps itself an exercise in denial: to avoid, by ignoring, negative feelings which really are there and which will find, eventually, a way of making their pres-ence felt.

Our sense of what is normal (our horizon of expect-ation) is crucial to our capacity to cope with difficulty. If we take it for granted that certain difficulties are going to come our way we do not find that their awkwardness is reduced, but we do avoid a secondary level of worry. The secondary worry – the one that really knocks us off course – is the panicky voice which shouts out: I thought I loved this person, but now I'm miserable, it's all over, our love is finished. This is like the despair that prevents people from writing. Perhaps the most poignant know-ledge the artist can acquire is of the vicissitudes of cre-ation. People who want to write sometimes get down a few pages only to give up in dismay when, rereading what they have written, it strikes them as hopelessly bad.

The seasoned writer may be just as appalled when reading through a first draft. But with this difference: they have limited expectations of a first draft; they know that it is only that and they know that it can be improved. This is not a difference at the level of propositions, for the person who gives up might intellectually assent to the point I have just made. Only it doesn't carry through into their drives, ambitions and efforts. The horizon of expectation is different – the assumption about what sort of obstacles will arise allows one person to go on when another gives up. Love, in relation to ambivalence, has its own vicissitudes. Our recognition that these are inevitable – and indeed an internal part of love – allows them to seem less a reason to give up. And, of course, the same point applies in our sense of those we love. That they sometimes turn on us with what seems like a cold annoyance, or say things which leave one wondering whether divorce proceedings should be instigated tomorrow or perhaps this afternoon, may be doing something which is very much part of the normal process of loving: finding that love itself provokes anxieties and fears, and reacting to these with aggression.

20

sexuality

The special moments when sexual desire and love come together and enhance one another have a privileged place in our imaginative lives. Such moments represent an ideal of being together – the fusion of two people. It is not just coyness which leads us to speak of 'making love' – sex can provide the most eloquent way of making passion evident. Because sexual passion is hard to fake, lust can be reassuring – it proves that two people still find each other attractive. Sex is direct, whereas love is diffuse. Sometimes we need love to be made obvious – and sex is one of the most powerful ways in which this can happen.

In the Courtauld Institute there is a small painting by Edouard Vuillard – a late follower of the Impressionists – depicting a naked woman retrieving a gown from the back of a chair. The large airy room in which we see her is clearly the artist's studio. The picture testifies to a complete ease between the painter and the woman. This beautiful image reminds us that sexuality isn't just about sex; it conveys a sense of trust and comfort which are connected to tender touch. This is the sensuality of a caress, rather than of intercourse. It is, as it were, the hinterland of sex which is most powerfully evocative of intimacy. Many people who feel intense jealousy at the thought of their partner having sex with another say that it is not intercourse itself which is the focus of their anguish, so much as what they imagine to come before and afterwards. It is these passages of sensual closeness which most directly tie sex to love.

On the other hand it is evident that sex and love often float apart. This is not surprising when we consider that they are, ultimately, two quite distinct parts of life. Sexuality is a comparatively narrow field of passion, intimately linked to physical excitement and orgasm. Lust – especially male lust – is often excited by obvious and rather impersonal attributes. This explains why, according to *Cosmopolitan*, you can make yourself more sexy by putting a little thought into your wardrobe – a recipe which can hardly be predicted to make you more lovable in the long run: the only run that counts, when it comes to love. Qualities which make someone lovable – such as patience, loyalty and cosiness – can even be liabilities when it comes to sexual appeal. And, of course, sexiness, especially in its most blatant versions, often promises nothing at all with respect to love.

There are basically two ways in which people have tried to suggest that sex and love can be brought into harmony. That is, there are two ways in which people have imagined that we can find satisfaction in sex and in love at the same time. One is the traditional Christian view that love is the proper basis of sex. According to this line of thought, real sexual satisfaction is possible only when we have sex with someone we love. Sex needs love because the goal of sex, its *telos*, is the expression of complete closeness between two people. Love ennobles sex; sex without love is degrading; it leaves us unhappy with ourselves; it leaves us feeling that we have behaved 'like animals'. In other words, sex is seen as an inherently emotional and moral activity, one which inescapably makes a romantic claim upon the partners. Sex involves spiritual as well as physical passion. Although we can, obviously, act on merely physical passion we cannot have a full and satisfying sexual life if we do so.

The alternative position, the second vision of how we can be happy in both sex and love, separates the two. Sex is regarded as no different from other physical pleasures: the enjoyment of food or sport, for example. Just as it would be absurd to suppose that you should only ever play tennis or have lunch with your lover so, the argument runs, it is absurd to think that you should only ever have sex with the person you love. If sex is merely a form of pleasant exercise it is wildly irrational to think that sexual fidelity has anything at all to do with love.

Each option recognizes something important. The Christian view accepts that we do invest sex with special moral and emotional significance not accorded to other activities and thinks that we are right to make this investment. It takes sexual jealousy very seriously. Since we are sexually possessive creatures we ought to build this into our morality, otherwise we shall be trying to efface a basic element of our sexual character. On the other hand, the view that sex is like tennis recognizes that sexual desire doesn't always coincide with love. So it wishes to abolish jealousy. The troubling fact is that both positions are correct. We are inherently jealous and sexual desire is distinct from love. To accept both claims is to admit a degree of incoherence in human nature. In the face of this incoherence there are really only two strategies we can adopt as we try to cope with this unfortunate condition. We can follow either the path of renunciation or the path of secrecy. Renunciation says that you have to abandon certain possibilities of sexual satisfaction in order to maintain love. Secrecy says that you have to take something away from love, namely honesty and openness, if you are to have sexual satisfaction. Whichever of these paths we follow, it is evident that each reveals a flaw in the ideal of love.

The ideal of love involves both harmony and honesty. Were we to find true love, we think, all of our longings and desires would come to focus on a single person. All the forces of our personality would be brought into harmony because they would all have the same object: the happiness of the beloved. Now it appears that this ideal is incompatible with a central feature of human nature. Sexual desire does not get corralled in this way. Even if we are emotionally committed to one person, our sexual instincts will continue to behave as if in ignorance of this commitment. It is as if the erogenous parts of our bodies just don't know very much about our current emotional lives. We also think that love involves honesty. We think that to love another person is, in part, to reveal ourselves fully to them. But sexuality undermines this ideal. It is asking too much of another person to invite them to accept the disloyal aspects of sexual desire; for this is asking them to switch off the tendency to possessiveness, something which it does not lie in their power to do.

It is not only because sexual desire can lead one of the partners to be unfaithful that it is in tension with love. Probably, for most people, the problem of how to have sex within a relationship is more pressing. And this is a psychologically prior issue, since usually people only have affairs because there is something important that they feel they cannot have with their current partner. And quite often this is to do with the kind of sex one of the partners wants to have.

Facing an apparently very different problem, Ruskin once remarked that the greatest contribution a duke could make to the modern world would be to take a job as a greengrocer. What lay behind this apparently bizarre suggestion was the following sequence of thoughts. Ruskin was concerned about the ideas his contemporary Victorians had as to what constituted a dignified life. Many people felt strongly that dignity was incompatible with being a small shopkeeper. But since a great many people did work in shops, such a way of thinking about dignity was both cruel and destructive. It cut many hard-working and decent people off from the respect of others and from self-respect. If, however, a duke were to take time off from breeding racehorses and attending the House of Lords to stand behind a counter, in the belief that supplying people with good vegetables at a fair price is an inherently worthwhile thing to do, then all this might begin to change. A prejudice about dignity might give way to a more reasonable assessment of worth. No one would be able to doubt the duke's dignity, so it would become apparent that one could be an individual worthy of the highest respect and also run a corner shop. Two things which had been radically opposed would come to be understood as compatible. And something very similar can be seen to apply to sex and love.

Much unhappiness comes about because we suppose that certain sexual desires cannot be expressions of love.

If our partner wants to do *that* they cannot be lovable and they cannot be loving. Ruskin's point didn't just concern how others judge shopkeepers. He wanted shopkeepers to take their own dignity more seriously. With sex both perspectives matter. It is not just that one's partner may think what one wants to do is disgusting; one may join in with this denunciation. Of course, some actions really are incompatible with love, just as some ways of living really do rob people of dignity. But the interesting cases occur when we are too quick to think that an act is unloving or a job degrading.

Ruskin is inviting us to be more imaginative about dignity. He is inviting us to move from a prejudice to a question; from the assumption that selling vegetables must be degrading to a question about the real nature of dignity. It is the same imaginative move that we often need to make with respect to sex. It can seem as if this is a point addressed only to women; for often it is the woman who reacts negatively to the man's suggestion in bed. But, in fact, the issue is more symmetrical than this. For the equation runs in two directions. If, following Ruskin, we can see that being a vegetable seller isn't necessarily degrading, we can equally come to see that being a racehorse breeder or a member of the House of Lords is not a sure guarantee of high human worth, or of dignity. And a point with the same structure is often relevant to the way men see women as sexually appealing. A man may need to be more imaginative, may need to widen his sense of what is sexually attractive.

The tensions between love and sex cannot be made to disappear; but reading a little Ruskin may help to take the worst bitterness out of the tragedy of the bedroom.

love's increase

Although the general experience of mankind attests to the decline of all our personal loves, there seems to be a rarer – but still real – possibility of love growing over time and becoming stronger and deeper. But how does love increase? Shakespeare famously toys with the idea that music can feed love but does not tell us what kind of music he has in mind. Ironically – if we take the suggestion seriously – it seems more plausible to assign such a potency not to the pieces which seek to convey love's intensity (as in the rapturous duets of Tristan and Isolde) but to works which, at first sight, have no connection with love at all. We may find that the sonorous, sad phrases of the slow fifth movement of Beethoven's late String Quartet, Opus 130, put us in a frame of mind in which we feel we appreciate love. When the broad, deep strokes of the cello give way to a lighter passage of hesitant tenderness, we may – as we absorb ourselves in the emotive atmosphere of the music – find that a longing to love and be loved takes hold.

To shed light on this phenomenon we might start with a crude analogy. It is a general psychological law that we only appreciate good things when their use is apparent. During the summer we give hardly a thought to our winter coat. But a cold autumn morning can bring a relish for its warm protection. It takes a vivid apprehension of a chill wind to makes us feel the pleasure of wearing such a heavy garment. So too with more subtle feelings. A minor act of tenderness – a hand stretching out at night, a consoling smile, a slight pause when someone listens carefully – may make very little impression upon us when we feel buoyant and well able to look after ourselves. But such gestures look quite different when perceived against a more sombre or hostile backdrop. What the music of Beethoven can do is draw us into an awareness of the basic sorrow of existence; from the point of view of one who is absorbed in the music, life looks like an assemblage of vain preoccupations and delusions through which the sounds of the strings break. And when we feel this, those small indications of kindness and warmth come to look like the most precious things life has to offer. It is just this move which is widely used in literature and film to make us see the power of small acts of generosity. In Theodor Fontane's haunting novel *Effi Briest*, for example, we may find, towards the end, that we are moved to tears by a simple letter Effi's doctor writes to her parents recommending that, as she is unwell, she come and stay with them in the country. Hardly moving, of course, when considered in isolation. But that's the whole point. Effi, who in the early sections of the novel is abundantly energetic and hopeful, has been rejected by society – and her parents – because of a brief affair she has had in the first year of her marriage. The doctor's letter is therefore to be seen against a background of callousness and righteous judgement. His kindness is just that he to continues to care for Effi when everyone else has turned from her. But we feel that quiet kindness intensely when we are brought face to face with how easily others leave her to drift.

The feeling that the music or the novel engenders – a feeling of appreciation for small acts of kindness – may be termed katabasis, a going down. It is worth dignifying it with a special name because, although generally unremarked, it is one of the most significant and valuable movements of consciousness that art can achieve. It is a counterpart of the famous notion of the sublime, in which we come to an ecstatic self-awareness. In the moment of katabasis we come down from the ordinary plateau of indifference, we recognize the dark background of existence – its loneliness, disappointment, fragility – and from here we see clearly just how much we really need (like the emerging melody) the hesitant tenderness of another person. It is not suffering as such that makes someone appreciate love, it is only when suffering pierces our vanity – which happens when we do not blame someone else for our pain – that it awakens a deeper respect for love.

Katabasis is essentially dialectical. That is, it is a movement from a habitual state of complacency to an admission of emotional vulnerability. It would be wrong, therefore, to think harshly of complacency – which, for much of the time, is a perfectly good state to be in. Life would be unbearable if we were permanently in a katabatic condition; in Beethoven's Opus 130 the movement lasts only a few minutes before we are passed on to a more lively finale. The deepening of love – the increased appreciation of what another person has to offer us, what they are to us – occurs when we hold on to the import of these passages; when we return to them often enough.

*

Katabasis – the moment of humility – belongs to a class of virtues which we might call 'recuperative'. These are the capacities to recover from the things which undermine love. Our capacity, for example, to forgive something the beloved has done; to accept a wrong we have done them. Recuperation is essential to the survival of love because it is inevitable that love will come up against serious difficulties.

Every theory of love works with a vision of what can go wrong in life. We have already seen how love is connected to the need to overcome isolation. Indeed it is this which Erich Fromm makes central to *The Art of Loving*. He argues, there, that love is the only thing which can fully connect us to another person – and since being disconnected from other people is, he thinks, the central problem of our times, love is the solution to the key problem of human existence. The emphasis on recuperation which I am arguing for here is not a disavowal of Fromm's thesis, but a supplement to it. (One can think that loneliness is a big problem, without claiming that it is the only problem.) The point is that even within a good relationship there are continual sources of hurt and disappointment which have to be overcome if love is to survive; their overcoming is actually the growth and development of love. It is, therefore, extremely important that we work with a vision of love which sees problems not as the end of love, not as a sign that love is over, but as the ground upon which love operates.

This is why a forgiving attitude to another person is an essential element of love. Love is destroyed when we hold on to the image of the other as blameworthy, as guilty of having wronged us. Forgiveness relies upon adopting a point of view from which their actions or words can be seen as expressions of their own suffering rather than just as malicious. Thus the loving eye may see a vicious remark as a sign of that person's vulnerability, as an indication of weakness. To such an eye, the action calls less for revenge or defence than for compassion. Of course, this is exceedingly hard to achieve. This ideal of love seeks to see past the surface of behaviour and look at the causes of such conduct. Central to this conception of love is the idea that the loving person needs, just as much, to meet with this kind of response. Such love is based on the belief that I too stand in need of forgiveness from the other and that is why I am ready to forgive.

maturity

In the earlier parts of this book we looked at some of the things which draw people into love. We delineated the needs of the lover and the way imagination functions to build up the impression that another will be able to satisfy those needs. We considered the way in which imagination gives us an image of the beloved which fills them with good things and, for a time, allows their least quality to take on an extraordinary charm and force in our eyes. We have dwelt upon the ideal of care, in which we think of ourselves as being able to perform some fundamental good for the other. But it is obvious that all of these things – the things which take us into love – are, by their nature, subject to disappointment. The image our imagination has created must inevitably be undermined by continuous close contact with the one we love. We will be forced to recognize our impotence in the face of their problems, we will have to confront the limits of our understanding of them (the moment when they turn and say: 'You really don't understand', or when they behave in ways which contravene our assumptions about their character – when the girl one thought was full of confidence comes home night after night with her spirits dashed by the difficulties of the day). We will have to face the moment when we feel that we are misunderstood, or when we feel our lover's needs as intrusive. We may feel we are being judged according to an alien standard – when a man judges his partner by reference to his mother, a woman by reference to her father. Intense fascination can give way to boredom and predictability.

Away from the romantic sphere you will have to confront the point when a child turns and says 'I don't like you', or seems uninterested in communicating with you, or (even more difficult) when you are faced with your own resentments against your child ('You have stolen my life'). All this is only too familiar.

In one of the most compelling of his many studies of relationships, *Family Happiness*, Tolstoy takes us through the early years of a fairly unremarkable marriage. A middle-aged man, Sergey, and a younger woman, Masha, meet in the country; the story is related in her voice. He is an old family friend who has managed the financial affairs of the young woman and her sister since the deaths of their parents. Gradually, hardly noticing what is happening, she falls in love with him. Tolstoy's artistry is never more finely displayed than when he conveys, with such apparent artlessness, the small steps by which such a great change is accomplished in Masha's inner life. One evening she is playing the piano:

> He sat behind me, where I could not see him; but everywhere – in the half darkness of the room, in every sound, in myself – I felt his presence. Every look, every movement of his, though I could not see them, found an echo in my heart.

He is just as much in love with her and this mutual rapture continues after they marry. 'He alone existed on earth for me and I considered him the best and most faultless man in the world; so that I could not live for anything else in the world other than for him.' Tolstoy beautifully depicts the happy details of their life together – their laughter-filled breakfasts, their evenings of music, their intimate midnight suppers. Gradually we hear notes of conflict and disillusion. After two months of married life, in spite of his company,

I began to feel lonely, that life was repeating itself, that there was nothing new either in him or in myself. He began to give more time to business which kept him away from me and I began to feel that there was a special department of his mind into which he was unwilling to admit me. His unbroken calmness provoked me. Another new and disturbing sensation began to creep into my heart. To love him was not enough for me after the ecstasy I had felt in falling in love. I wanted movement and not a calm course of existence. I knew there was noise and glitter and excitement elsewhere and hosts of people suffering and rejoicing without one thought for us and our remote existence.

She is irritated by his calm manner, which she starts to interpret as veiled aggression: that he seeks to humiliate her with his 'majestic composure'. They go to St Petersburg to bring more excitement into her life; she is a social success and throws herself into a season of balls and grand parties, although 'he was evidently bored and wearied by the life we were leading. I was too busy, however, to think of that.' And so we are shown their mounting dissatisfaction with one another and, of course, the many moments of misunderstanding, the many failures of communication, which lead to a complete breakdown in their relationship. They continue to live together for several years, but pursuing separate lives. They have two children, but this does not bring them closer. While their own house is having some work done on it, they go to stay for a time in her childhood home, where her romance with Sergey had started – and at the same season of the year. On seeing again the things which had so enchanted her when she was first in love, Masha finds herself reflecting on the passage of time:

Where were those visions now? All that I had hardly dared to hope when I was a girl had come to pass. My vague confused dreams had become a reality, and the reality had become an oppressive, difficult and joyless life. All remained the same at the old house – the garden through the window, the grass, the path, the very same bench above the dell, the same song of the nightingale by the pond, the same lilacs in full bloom, the same moon shining about the house; and yet in everything such a terrible, inconceivable change! Such coldness in all that might have been near and dear! . . . Am I the same woman, but without love or the desire for love, with no longing for work and no content within myself?

It is in these reflections that she feels most vividly what she has been feeling in a vague a way for a long time – that her old love and self are dead. Masha feels a second burden on top of this, deriving from the interpretation she places on her feeling. She thinks that she is responsible for the end of their love or, perhaps, that her husband could have saved it if he had not been so distant, as she feels he has been. Their love could have survived and they are, in her eyes, guilty of destroying it. She by reckless seeking after excitement, he by complacent withdrawal. Their love has died; someone must be guilty.

In a desperate attempt to set things right she puts these thoughts to her husband. But he suggests a different way of looking at what has happened, seeing it as inevitable, even as benign. The old love had to die in order to make way for something else, so no one is to blame, no one has anything to be sorry for in this change. And the change had to be difficult because it is necessary to come to terms (he says) with one's own longings and to burn them up by pursuing them. 'All of us must have personal experience of all the nonsense of life in order to get back to life itself; the evidence of other people is no good.'

I looked at him and suddenly my heart grew light; it seemed that the cause of my suffering had been removed like an aching nerve. Suddenly I realized clearly and calmly that the past feeling, like the past time itself, was gone beyond recall, and that – were it even possible – it would be painful and uncomfortable to bring it back.

She has grown up.

That day ended the romance of our marriage; the old feeling became a precious, irrecoverable remembrance; but a new feeling of love for my children and the father of my children laid the foundation of a new life and a quite different happiness; and that life and happiness have lasted to the present time.

Tolstoy has told us the story of a particular relationship. As recounted, its details depend on the individual characters delineated: he is older, rather self-contained and imperturbable; she is young, ardent and entranced, for several years, by a glamorous social life. But the power of the tale does not rest only in its account of the conflict and eventual resolution of these two individuals. It carries with it a suggestion of something much more general: a thesis about the nature of maturity. It suggests that we are all, at some stage, prey to hopes and restless, vague yearnings for fulfilment: 'all the nonsense of life' Sergey calls it – unfairly. Unfairly, because this impossible yearning is the precondition of the opening phase of love, in which the beloved can seem utterly wonderful and life blissful. It is only 'nonsense' in that it expects and hopes too much from life. So it is destined to burn itself out. This is traumatic and we have to face it for ourselves – no reports from the other side can help us. But, if we are fortunate, we will eventually see that this trauma was not our own fault, nor the fault of our partner. We come to inhabit a different perspective upon life; we no longer think that it is possible – if only we were sweeter, if only our partner were more understanding or more passionate – to sustain the delights of the opening stage of the relationship. Once we have accepted this we are relieved from a burden of guilt as well as from debilitating expectations; we can then come back to the business of getting on with life, of appreciating whatever good things we have actually managed (despite ourselves) to amass. Masha has a pleasant home, two healthy children, a good-natured, intelligent husband; she has a taste and aptitude for music and the business of their estate to take an active interest in. These things are not exciting but, when seen with an appreciative eye, they are adequate for a happy life.

We could say, in short, that Tolstoy has told us the story of a woman coming to maturity. Her first love was intense and delightful, but immature. Her subsequent sufferings have brought her to a mature outlook. We often use the word 'mature' in a fairly casual sense; it is one of those general psychological terms – like 'deep' or 'wise' – which can seem to fall to pieces in our hands when we try to pin a more definite sense upon it, when we try to spell out just what it is we want to capture with the word. One of the things which philosophy can do is to try to flesh out, with as much precision as the case allows, just what is at stake in the concepts we use. And this task is, obviously, all the more important when we come to the concepts we most rely upon in thinking about life. (And we may say that whoever seriously attempts such a task is, *ipso facto*, a philosopher.) Perhaps the reason why maturity is hard to pin down is that it functions both as a term for getting older and for a certain kind of psychological achievement. We use it to describe age and an elusive moral virtue. It posits some crucial relationship between the two, but clearly it would be a mistake to see this as a simple connection.

The term 'mature' carries certain negative connotations when it comes to love. Sometimes we use it to imply caution and a lack of spontaneity; it involves wanting to be safe rather than sorry. In line with this, the 'mature' individual would be sceptical about other people's motives and unimpressed by passion. In this sense, it is not at all a romantic conception. The great lovers, the romantic heroes, are not at all 'mature'. Imagine Byron, Romeo or even Hamlet being prudent, self-controlled, conservative in their expectations. We can understand this if we look back and consider what draws people into love in the first place, what the conditions for falling in love are. This involves passionate yearning for something we believe the other can give us; it involves an imaginative process of endowing the other with a set of exaggerated qualities which make them appear wonderful in our eyes. It involves believing that we have found the 'perfect other'. None of this is compatible with the conservative and reasonable outlook we characterize as mature.

Isn't this just what Tolstoy has tried to show us? The experience of love has to begin outside of maturity; it's just that, if a relationship is to last, if love is to survive and develop over an extended period, we need to bring to the relationship a set of qualities quite different from those which took us into it in the first place. The Byronic hero might be madly exciting to have an affair with, but would be a nightmare as a husband. Imagine Hamlet as a father. Imagine Cathy discussing mortgage repayments with Heathcliff. This is the internal tragedy of love. If love is successful, if our love is returned and develops into a relationship, the person we are with must turn out to be other than we imagined them to be. Love craves closeness, and closeness always brings us face to face with something other than we expected. The person who looked so confident and full of life when we knew them at first turns out, eventually, to have an array of hidden anxieties and fears. Security can put us off our guard. We were witty and attentive when we were trying to win someone's affection; once we have it we may return to a different model of behaviour. When love is successful it leads to a new set of actions – children, buying property, sharing domestic responsibility; coping even moderately well with these requires a different set of qualities from those which may have incited our love in the first place. (Of course, if these prudential characteristics had been uppermost in our minds as we got together with someone, this would hardly be described as 'falling in love'.) The trajectory of love necessarily requires some development in the attitudes and feelings of the lovers.

'Maturity' is at its most potent as a contrastive term. We see certain episodes of behaviour, or certain personality traits (in ourselves or in others) as profoundly defective. There is something amiss with a person who is always on the defensive, who experiences anything less than flattering comment as a personal attack. Every morning I make resolutions which I break every evening, I pass from regret to impulse to regret. I am crippled with envy and never get on with making a go of my own resources and opportunities. I always blame others for whatever goes wrong in my life. I imagine that everyone is much better (or much worse) than me. If we call these attitudes and ways of behaving 'immature' we are tacitly appealing to a positive notion of maturity, to a vision of personality in which we could be comparatively free from these problems. In this respect we see the necessity of a word which will try to draw together a group of characteristics which are central to a reasonable account of the capacity to cope with the problems of existence; a term which will delineate the overcoming of a range of very understandable problems with ourselves and other people with which most of us begin our adult lives.

The notion of maturity is humanity's attempt to retain an optimistic picture of love in the face of disappointment and difficulty. Maturity is an ideal – as much as it is an observation of the resolutions some people come to of the difficulties of existence. The core of maturity lies in the idea of learning from experience. But learning what? One thing which we might hope to learn is how to settle our priorities and to accept the trade-offs that are necessary for the pursuit of our goals. It is mature to recognize that you have to pick your fights, conserve your forces, and accept limits on what you can achieve. Thus it would be mature to accept a certain plainness in one's partner if they possess more important qualities such as a sweet temper or reliability.

Contrast this qualified optimism with the much more negative vision of experience which is expounded in Lampedusa's tragic novel, *The Leopard*. Towards the close of the novel, the old prince is watching his favourite nephew dance with a beautiful young woman, whom he is shortly to marry. We know already that they will not be happy together; they will in no way refute the prince's maxim that marriage is a year of fire and thirty years of ashes. But as they dance, they are magnificent.

They were the most moving sight there, two young people in love dancing together, blind to each other's defects, deaf to the warnings of fate, deluding themselves that the whole course of their lives would be as smooth as the ballroom floor, unknowing actors set to play the parts of Juliet and Romeo by a director who had concealed the fact that the tomb and the poison were already in the script. Neither was good, each self-interested, each turgid with secret aims, yet there was something sweet and touching about them both; those murky but ingenuous ambitions of theirs were obliterated by the words of jesting tenderness he was murmuring in her ear, by the scent of her hair, by the mutual clasp of those bodies destined to die.

Here experience does not add up. We do not, according to this account, pass through our mistakes to emerge stronger and more settled. The perspective which time brings to the perceptive individual is not a consoling one. Happiness is fleeting, we can only reconnect with it in regarding the brief illusions of the young. The illusion is touching, but it is not the immature version of a future stable satisfaction; it is a momentary relief from the appalling spectacle of existence.

In the bleak light of Lampedusa's vision, we can see that Tolstoy, in the end, gives a rather one-sided account of maturity. He rightly sees it as involving a certain grasp and acceptance of the larger patterns of life. But in the story we have been examining he breaks off too soon. Before, that is, having to deal with the possibility that the clear-eyed look at life might end up seeing something too grim to be accepted with any equanimity. There is a maturity in the prince's outlook – a maturity of perspective which sees life as a whole – but it doesn't bring him any comfort.

Maturity is our name for the hopeful strategy which is open to us when faced with something which is both an object of high value (a source of happiness) and, at the same time, threatening, difficult, disturbing. The very things which draw us into love and enable us to invest so highly in another person, to wish to bind our lives together, themselves give rise to disillusionment, frustration, disappointment, and evoke some of our deepest fears and most primitive defences. What we mean by maturity is a change of perspective. Expectations are reduced, and one judges not by what is desired but by what it is possible to obtain. We desire the perfect counterpart of our soul, the person who will always understand and respond. All we can actually get is someone who is, intermittently, pretty sympathetic and fairly interested and understanding – provided they have not had a hard day. But the whole point of maturity is that this change in perspective is not an intellectual shift. It is so easy to assent to this change of expectation as a good idea – maturity is not the idea but the actual reduction of expectation. That is why we fear as well as desire maturity.

In this book I have tried to argue two things – each argument runs through the book as a whole. Firstly, the need to love and to be loved is deeply placed in human nature. It springs from certain inherited evolutionary characteristics but it is also bound up with much more recent developments of self-consciousness: we long to be understood, to be close to another person, to matter in another's life. These concerns may have had some rudimentary presence in the lives of our remotest ancestors, but they have been massively increased, and brought to the foreground of experience, only in recorded history. And because they are aspects of culture, they vary to some degree from society to society – as these needs are variously interpreted. It is, however, precisely the same factors – the factors which draw us into love – that constitute the roots of love's difficulties. We long to be understood, but it is often awkward to have another see too much of one's inner troubles. We try to be charitable, but we are susceptible to boredom and impatience. Above all, we do not go through life with a strictly coherent set of desires, and anyone who charms us in one frame of mind may be annoying in another.

Secondly, love is an achievement, it is something we create, individually, not something which we just find, if only we are lucky enough. But although it is a creation and an achievement it is not something which can be forced simply by effort. You can't just sit down and decide to love someone and, through doing this, find that you do really love them. This is unsurprising if we reflect that love is dependent upon many other achievements: kindness of interpretation, sympathy, understanding, a sense of our own needs and vulnerability. And these kinds of capacity and awareness do not spring suddenly into being. Each requires patient cultivation: we have to take whatever fragile presence each has in our lives and build upon that. If this is true of loving it is also true of being lovable. Being lovable cannot really be separated from being a good person in general. There seem to be counter-instances in which physical attractiveness or glamour make individuals the target of love. But it is obvious that these characteristics play a much smaller role in generating a love that lasts – one which can weather the inevitable periods of disenchantment and dissatisfaction on both sides. In our culture we have become rather disinclined to pay attention to individual responsibility in loving. We place too much emphasis on finding the right person and not nearly enough upon the cultivation of qualities which allow us to deserve love and which enable us to give love – even when things are difficult.

'There are people who would never have fallen in love if they had never heard others talking about it.' So writes La Rochefoucauld in a celebrated maxim (no. 136) with the painful implication that the reader may belong to this class, the class of people who cannot love properly.

It is not hard to be sympathetic to the spirit of maxim 136. La Rochefoucauld is reminding us how self-deception can enter into even the most esteemed emotions. The passion is trumped up; it is put on for the sake of a flattering self-image: 'I too am a lover; I belong to the spiritual élite.' We could replace 'fallen in love' with 'a passion for the work of Van Gogh' (or 'for snowboarding') and the phrase would retain its bite.

Pitifully, for the history of thought, any single good point can obscure something else which we need to bear in mind. Maxim 136 encourages us to amalgamate two very different kinds of talk. There is a kind of talk (or writing, or film) which makes it seem exciting and fashionable to be in love and makes us want to be in love; but, crucially, it provides the wrong motive – vanity. On the other hand there is, perhaps, talk which helps to cultivate our capacity for love. Instead of functioning as an advertisement for love it might, for example, help us to unlock our passions, to recognize our need for another, to see our present loneliness.

There is an ambiguity of language which masks a critical difference. La Rochefoucauld writes: 'There are people who would never have fallen in love' – would never have been in what exactly? If he means 'love' in the limited sense of romantically dreamy about someone, then perhaps he is right. But if we take the term with its larger implications then the maxim falls apart. Can we imagine someone leading a life of devotion, tenderness, understanding and attachment to another merely because of some enticing talk they heard in the salon? Effect radically outstrips cause. Or we might ask what he means by 'talk'. Occasional chatter or insightful discussion sustained over years? But could the latter never produce more than fake excitement? Could so much yield only a worthless infatuation?

Unintentionally, perhaps, this famously cynical remark invites an optimistic interpretation. Seeking to remind us how superficial and gullible we are, it actually inspires, in anyone sitting down to write or read about love, an attractive hope. For it suggests that we might make a loving from a loveless life – if only we can find the right sort of talk.

index